PENGUIN BOOKS

SEEKING HOME

Amanda Oon is an editor, journalist, and author. She writes on social issues, lifestyle, and culture, with a focus on East–West connections.

SEEKING HOME

REFLECTIONS ON FAMILY, CULTURE, AND IDENTITY

AMANDA OON

PENGUIN BOOKS
An imprint of Penguin Random House

PENGUIN BOOKS

Penguin Books is an imprint of the Penguin Random House group of companies whose addresses can be found at global.penguinrandomhouse.com

Published by Penguin Random House SEA Pte Ltd
40 Penjuru Lane, #03-12, Block 2
Singapore 609216

Penguin Random House SEA

First published in Penguin Books by Penguin Random House SEA 2025

10 9 8 7 6 5 4 3 2 1

ISBN 9789815144055

Typeset in Garamond by MAP Systems, Bengaluru, India

www.penguin.sg

THE FAMILIAR UNFAMILIAR

Changi Airport

Our plane touches down at Changi airport.

If you haven't been to Singapore's Changi airport, picture it as the Marie Antoinette of airports. The Kim Kardashian of airports. This is the sort of airport that makes other airports want to have a midlife crisis and flush their pension on a Ferrari. There are many reasons why this transport hub consistently holds a spot among the World Airport Awards' Best Airports in the World. These include a butterfly garden, a 40-metre-high indoor waterfall, a sprawling rooftop canopy park, and a ten-storey shopping mall. There are also immigration counters and an arrivals hall for mundane airport things like international travel.

Singapore is a land of dreams. The legendary prince who first landed on its shores thought he saw a majestic lion, naming the island 'Singapura', Lion City, before he discovered there were no maned felines around here. The fable inspired another fantasy, the Merlion, a trippy half-leonine fish spewing water into the Marina Bay.

My husband Paul and I walk down the corridor to immigration, in tandem, like we walked down the aisle that afternoon in Maidenhead. We're considerably less well dressed for this new threshold, the next stage of our adventure. We pick up two fat suitcases and cart our physical and emotional baggage out into the wall of humid tropical air.

It is raining as we scoot towards the city, the road lined with palm fronds and the aptly-named Rain trees. This is one of the first misconceptions about Singapore—that it is always sun-soaked. It rains often, in short stints, two-hour-long sobbing gulps where the sky purges water down like a drunk emotional release. Deep monsoon drains turn into sprinting rivulets. After the rain, the city feels cool, clean, and slightly dazed, like it's woken up from a nap.

'This first time living in Singapore, boss?' asks the taxi driver ferrying us towards the city. Paul, who has never been called 'boss' by anyone in his life looks vaguely and politely confused.

'It's his first time,' I chirp helpfully. No one has ever called me 'boss' either, but I've had a lot of coffee on the plane. Plus, I'll answer to pretty much anything for a chat.

'And you, sister?'

'Me? No . . . my family are actually from around here. I've been here before. When I was very small . . .'

The driver glances at me in his rear-view mirror, taking in my unwashed face, my hair styled 'electric shock' chic, my faded T-shirt and baggy elephant pants from a holiday in Bali.

'You . . .' he says finally, 'still very small.'

Why People Move Countries

1. Because they have to. Because the tremors of conflict tearing cracks in their country have turned their home into your headline. And they cannot live as part of a headline so they become a statistic, displaced in numbers
2. Because they want to. Because the grass is always greener past someone else's borders. And there's the shining sell of the immigrant's dream advertising something more
3. For love
4. For money
5. For tax purposes
6. To find yourself
7. To lose yourself
8. For family
9. Because you are in your mid-thirties, and, as your friends move to the suburbs and start their own families, you're still teetering through a middle-class identity crisis, gazing at your navel to try and find a sense of belonging
10. Because your family has roots there, and moving haphazardly to a country you know almost nothing about because of a tentative family history seems a marginally better place to search for belonging than staring at your navel
11. For a job opportunity, the promises of an increasingly hyper-connected world, a 'global economy', 'digital nomadism'
12. To retire
13. To be closer to family
14. To be further from family

15. To start a family
16. To meet new people
17. To unnerve these new people with unexpected conversations about heritage, race, and belonging
18. Because somewhere in the depths of your belly, something is telling you have to do this
19. Because you want to fill your belly with new flavours and foods
20. For an education
21. For all the things you want to unlearn
22. To reinvent yourself
23. To rediscover yourself
24. To die
25. To fight
26. To live

Settling In

Our new home has windows that overlook the sequined lights of the central business district. It also has a 'bomb shelter', a boxy thick-walled enclave that has been a mandatory requirement for all new apartments since 1997. Protective trenches that can shield you from a shrapnel attack have been around the city since the Japanese occupation in the forties. Ours becomes a dumping-ground-and-walk-in-wardrobe, a sort of precaution against invasion that gives *Sex in the City* vibes.

Our new home is in Chinatown. The word reminds me of rows of gaudy red lanterns stretched across rain-soaked streets in Soho. It is where tourists go to scout out dumplings in London and where the city's Chinese immigrants have formed a tight-knit community around takeaways and other small businesses sitting cheek by jowl with the occasional betting shop and Pizza Express. Every major city has a Chinatown. There is a comforting universality about it, a reassurance that you know what to expect.

This Chinatown is different. This Chinatown is not an afterthought in the back streets of the city centre. This Chinatown *is* the city centre. It is the largest historical district in Singapore, sprawling across four sub-districts: Telok Ayer, Kreta Ayer, Bukit Pasoh, and Tanjong Pagar. There are wide open-air fruit stalls filling the streets with the pungent smell of rich, spiky durian. By the towering gables of the Buddha Tooth Relic Temple and Museum and the bright Lego-like squares of Chinatown Complex, teams of older Chinese uncles band together in hours-long, high-intensity mahjong tournaments.

There is a Daoist temple at the top of our street and a sex shop down the road.

Singapore's Chinatown was laid out by a white man. When Sir Stamford Raffles, the controversial colonial founder of the country, developed his blueprint of the state, he designated this area west of the river as a Chinese settlement, in the hopes that the growing numbers of immigrants arriving from mainland China would settle and grow the community and economy.

The Cantonese took Temple Street. The Teochews settled around South Canal Road and Garden and Carpenter Streets. And the Hokkiens established a base in Telok Ayer Street, where the gilded, dragon-decked rafters of Thian Hock Keng, Singapore's oldest Hokkien temple, now hosts a café and a small music box museum. Later that century, Indian and Malay settlers also filtered into the district, scattering their own cultures and religious hubs throughout the Chinese-dominated streets.

The Chinese immigrants came hungry for opportunities in this unknown new land. They made a living as coolie labourers in the stifling heat or as rickshaw drivers ferrying the wealthy until their backs and legs gave out. They carried with them ambitions to work at the mines, ports, plantations, and construction sites sprouting up across this young city.

Some women wore the bright headgear of the *samsui* or *hong tou jin*—'red headscarf women'—who hailed predominantly from the Samsui area of the coastal province of Canton. Others took on the stern black-and-white outfit of the *majie*, Cantonese domestic helpers pledging themselves to celibacy and the sisterhood, working domestic jobs to send money back home.

Networks formed within these quarters. As more migrants fled economic hardship in South China during China's Qing Dynasty, secret societies formed loosely around shared neighbourhoods, dialects, or acquaintances back home. Familiarity is a soothing balm to a foreigner. We are, as a species, more tribal than perhaps we'd like to admit.

These underground networks knew about the fastest bullock carts; that Pagoda Street was where you could get the best opium; and that Sago Street was a hotspot for brothels but also for mortuaries, 'death houses' whose doors welcomed a continuous roster of corpses covered in white sheets as children played on the pavement outside. They lived next door to each other, gossiped together, fell out, and supported each other through illness, hardship, and death.

Soon Chinatown wasn't even just a quarter for the Chinese. The peppermint green towers and bulbous onion domes of Masjid Chulia—also known as Masjid Jamae or Periya Palli 'Big Mosque'—and the piercing blue and green stained windows of Kuchu Palli 'Hut Mosque' Al-Abrar, which began life as a thatched hut, are some of the city's first Islamic halls of prayer. Sri Mariamman Temple, with its ornate six-tiered *gopuram* decked with colourful mythological statues, is Singapore's oldest Hindu temple.

In our first month, Paul and I watch a queue of barefoot men walk across a three-metre pit of smoking coals as part of the Theemithi fire-walking ceremony at the temple. Crowds, not just from the Hindu community, press together to watch participants hotfoot it towards the relative relief of a cool milk bath. Walking through intense heat for a blessing by the goddess Draupadi is a South Indian tradition. The teeth-gritting adrenaline rush of watching someone do something so painful makes your toes curl, possibly in empathy with the singed soles nearby.

There is a feeling I get walking through Chinatown—past the trunk-like pillars of the Chinese temples, through the basement wet market underworld of the Chinatown Complex, fizzing with activity and the smell of a hundred freshly slaughtered fish—of trampling on history. Of slipping my own foreign story into the cracks of a rich heritage building. But maybe that is what we're all doing in a way. The pastel coloured shophouses have turned into hipster cafés. The DIY shops lining Banda Street. The open-air market stalls hawking tourist tat and blasting Maroon 5 on Smith Street. The original southern Chinese settlers making Singapore their new home. Modern life stacked on top of history until the present becomes the past and so on, buried under new layers like a dim sum basket tower. Generations uprooting. Assimilating. Settling in.

Painting History

Painted figures watch you from the walls in this Chinatown. Here's a small boy in a Cantonese Opera beard sitting astride a letterbox. There's a man holding a massive teapot, pouring a stream of hot beverage from an open window. One day, I catch the artist in action. He is squatting, in cargo shorts, T-shirt, and wide brimmed sun hat, putting the finishing touches to a row of plump ducks hanging from a chef's wire, their bodies painted a ghostly white.

'There used to be ducks here,' he says pleasantly, when he catches me watching. 'Down there, right on this street. You could smell the meat. You could hear it cook. But they're long gone now.'

Yip Yew Chong has become a bit of a local celebrity. People watch him work. They take selfies against his painted walls, and he joins them, like an ink-stained rockstar flashing the victory sign at each iPhone lens. It's hard to believe that the fifty-four-year-old artist only started painting full-time in 2018, following a long career as an accountant.

Take care of business first, then follow your passion. This seems to be the Singaporean way. Maybe it is the interlocking network of traditional values that prioritize wealth and prosperity. Maybe it is an ingrained cultural cautiousness, fossilized generations deep in the cultural DNA. Or the social pressure of living in Asia's wealthiest country.

Maybe it's not just Singapore. There could be a kernel of truth in the cliché about 'respectable Asian careers'. Lil Sis and I stick out like two sore thumbs in our extended families, a Classicist and a History of Art graduate respectively, among a clan of finance professionals, with the occasional scientist or civil servant.

Now, more than fifty works decorate the city's public spaces in Yip's dreamlike signature style, bringing scenes from the nation's past into a modern urban environment. Walls at Woodlands look back through leafy depictions of quiet kampungs and gambier farms. A scene at the Rail Mall depicts the last train that ran across a corridor of now-disused tracks.

'Of course heritage is always important,' Yip replies when I ask him if he's chasing the past with his paint. It seems an obvious question. Heritage pours out with each brushstroke. Snapshots of Singapore's history appear in visions alongside backpacker's shops and boutiques.

'Actually, I never intended to create artwork with heritage themes,' he continues. 'My intent is to create artworks that reflect ways of life. But I had happy memories of my growing up years, so the visuals always look nostalgic.'

Four years on from this first meeting, the community will come out in its hundreds to celebrate the launch of a book celebrating Yip's life, *Art of Joy* by Woon Tai Ho. It charts his early childhood in Chinatown, his close family ties with his mother and grandmother, his move from corporate to creative, and the frightening and liberating importance of a second act. Yip will spend almost four hours on the first day continuously signing copies.

But for now, besides the tourist trying to insert her buttocks into a two-dimensional rattan chair for a photo, just how well-known and well-loved Yip and his art is, is temporarily muted. The crowds have dispersed and he is just a man, in baggy cargo shorts, a faded T-shirt, and a mocha-coloured sun hat, decorating a district with its own local memories.

Chinatown holds a special significance for Yip. He grew up on the second floor of a shophouse on Sago Lane, then a government (HDB) apartment block on Smith Street. His first exhibition was at the nearby Art Porters Gallery, after the owner found him immortalizing a Chinese *ah-mah* on Everton Road. Chinatown is where his most personal murals stand.

My Chinatown Home is a recreation of Yip's first family home, which is now a parking lot. Near the hanging ducks, Yip's mother cooks *nian gao*, the traditional New Year sticky cake, in the kitchen. His late seamstress grandmother sews a patchwork quilt in the living room. Yip explains how she sailed from Guangdong to Singapore as a teenager, where she met Yip's grandfather. He had dealings in the buzzing opium trade, and when the

British government cracked down on drugs in the fifties, he was forced to escape to China, where he died. Yip's newly-widowed grandmother worked two shifts to survive: a rubber factory during the day and scrubbing ships at night.

Chinatown's history is speckled with these stories: single women taking up the mantle of independence, juggling family and labour like a samsui woman's water buckets on either end of a wobbly shoulder pole.

On the shared wooden bed, a young Yip plays with his siblings.

'It's not just about remembering history. It's an intangible force that connects, harmonizes, and unifies a place,' current Yip says. He has managed to unify time periods. The dreamlike scenes from the sixties don't look a second out of place among the frenetic activity of today's Chinatown. They merge into the everyday—public, open, and visible.

'This type of art is accessible', Yip explains. 'You don't always have to go to a private home or gallery. It's very compelling to tell the story on the streets, and people feel like they can go any time.'

Sometimes, we need the past drawn out for us, in black and white, or gentle coloured brush strokes, to remind us who we used to be, how far we've come.

'People feel a sense of belonging if they know who they are and where they come from,' Yip says.

Belonging is knowing where you come from. Sometimes, I wonder, in our family's continued nomadic quest for 'home', whether each move is taking us further and further from our roots, if that is where we've taken a wrong turn.

The crowds have gone by the morning. The slope of Ann Siang Hill is empty apart from a few early risers doing Tai Chi on a tilt. Sounds of metal shutters opening like morning stretches filter through the Chinatown Complex market. On a stone table outside, a couple of elderly men share a silent pack of cigarettes. In a few hours, the square will come alive. In a deserted alley, the young painted Yip grins out at an empty audience. Below him hangs a drawing: a happy stick figure family and a pot with a paintbrush.

Yip is branching out from wall art. He likes its impermanence, the slow fade of paint rubbed off by years of life and weather, but says, 'There are too many murals now.' He is experimenting with digital art, immortalizing heritage in pixels.

'We've progressed,' he tells me simply, wiping his paintbrush and adding the final touches to his butchered ducks. 'Of course, we've lost some traditions. [And] we modified some into what we practise today. The spirit is still there, we miss it, but it's evolved. We don't cling onto the past.'

Minority to Majority

In Singapore, I am an ethnic majority. The tables have turned. I am in a country where around 75 per cent of people look a little bit like me.

Being in the majority sneaks up on you. There is something subconsciously comforting about the familiarity of a sea of dark hair and features that vaguely resemble yours joining you in the swarm of commuters that descend into the metro. There is something strangely reassuring about the fact that the prime minister and the majority of his cabinet look a bit like they could be uncles at your extended family gatherings. Representation matters. And here I am represented by over three quarters of the population.

Paul, on the other hand, is part of the resident Caucasian population of less than 3 per cent.[1]

'I'm the minority now,' he quips cheerfully. 'I guess I'll get to know what it feels like.'

He is wrong and he knows it. Being a white man in Singapore is not a typical ethnic minority experience. Many are expats, coasting through on a temporary stay of two, five, or twenty years, here on international visas. They work in white-collar jobs in flourishing sectors—finance, technology, and shipping are among some of the biggest Singaporean industries. This is the difference between an expat and a migrant worker: the wages and the colour of your skin.

There are ethnic minorities in Singapore: the Malays who make up around 13.5 per cent of the resident population,[2] the Indians who make up around 9 per cent, and the Eurasians and other groups joining Paul in the tiny 'other' category. Singapore is a proudly multiracial country. There are interracial harmony festivals and a national Racial Harmony Day, an uneasy commemoration of past racial riots. Government-subsidized public housing estates have carefully distributed race quotas to avoid ethnic enclaves. Race is a subject broached so conscientiously that it is at the forefront of everyone's identity; as part of the CMIO (Chinese, Malay, Indian, 'Other') classification system, where citizens are categorized by race to inform government policies, the ethnicity of every Singaporean is printed in black and white on their ID card.

But beneath this carefully constructed racial harmony, it is hard to ignore the fact that in an average Singaporean household, the median household income per member of a Chinese family in 2020 was still over $1,000 higher than that of a Malay family.[3] It's hard to unhear a deputy prime minister saying that he doesn't believe that Singapore is ready for a non-Chinese prime minister, even if the country's president later claimed it was.[4] And it's uncomfortable to take on board the inconvenient truths that come with being a majority.

I have heard the term 'Chinese privilege'. I have heard it raised, then dismissed by fervent advocates of the mantra that Singapore is a country built on meritocracy. I have heard a theory that the term itself is a post-colonial hangover, a projection of the term 'white privilege'. But I have never really thought about what it means before. When privilege is reflected back at you in the mirror, or in the reassuring mass of people who look like you, there aren't many reasons to consider or confront it.

'What is Chinese privilege?' I ask my friend Filzah, who comes from a conservative Malay Muslim family.

'Let me paint you a picture,' says Fil.

'Let's say I'm a Chinese person, with the right Chinese name, from the right Chinese family. And if my parents are quite well-off, they are friends with people who are quite well-off and all of them have kids that go to the same schools like Anglo-Chinese School or Raffles Institution. They are golfing buddies with COOs and CEOs and other high-flying corporate executives. And they all go to the same church, and the best schools, the best universities, and so on. So, when we talk about Chinese privilege, it's not really just about being part of a majority race. It's because of your race that you are part of an environment where you're set up to succeed because you are surrounded by other people who are successful.'

Chinese privilege is, according to Fil, being the token Malay in a meeting room or at a conference—even in a gym or yoga studio. It's the job applications where she has to worry that the hiring manager on a predominantly-Chinese staff might brush over her Malay sounding name. It's a meritocratic rat-race tailored to values not generally aligned with traditional Malay ideals, which, she says, centre on family life more than socio-economic hustle.

'What is Chinese privilege?' I ask my fun-loving, animal-loving friend Venky, who is from Tamil Nadu on his mother's side, Andhra Pradesh on his father's side, but born and brought up in the Lion City, third and fourth generation 'True Blue' Singaporean.

Chinese privilege is, according to Venky, when every business lunch or dinner at the agency where he works is a Chinese banquet. It's seeing the names of condominiums repeated in Chinese characters under the English name. It's when English movies are screened at the cinema with Chinese subtitles but never Tamil or Malay. It's the Special Assistance Plan schools, catering to academically-gifted students that admit predominantly Chinese pupils and teach bilingual English–Mandarin curriculums.

'It's feeling excluded from conversations that take place in the mother tongue of the majority. Feeling like I need to consciously behave in a certain way to avoid behaviours being justified by existing racial stereotypes. It's feeling conscious about speaking in Tamil to *prata* shop waiters when I'm with Chinese friends.'

This sort of racial inequality goes deeper than off-hand comments from members of parliament or well-intentioned promises of inter-ethnic harmony. It is ingrained in a system where everyone is set up to succeed, but some are set up to succeed more than others.

It seeps into the digital walls of the rental websites that place stern warnings like 'No Indian tenants please'. It rings through the testimonies I read in magazines of women of colour who grew up always feeling 'a little too hairy, a little too brown', of never 'seeing myself reflected positively in images anywhere in this country'. It is in the parody video made by Indian

Singaporean rapper Subhas Nair, accusing Chinese people of 'fucking it up' in response to an advertisement featuring Chinese actors in brownface.

Nair and his sister Preeti Nair, who collaborated with him on the video, received a two year 'conditional warning' from authorities.[5] But Nair was later charged in 2021 after making further race-related comments on social media, including statements alleging that Chinese Singaporeans received more lenient treatment after wrongdoing than Indian or Malay Singaporeans—a charge the government denied.[6]

Nair was was sentenced to six weeks in jail for 'promoting ill will' between racial and religious groups.[7]

It runs in the half-serious stereotypes thrown around lightly because everyone knows it is just banter. Indians are smelly. Malays are lazy. Asian women who love white men are gold-diggers, white men are here to steal our women and our jobs. Even the *ang mohs* don't get away totally free. Maybe Paul wasn't as wrong as he thought.

There was a book that came out a while ago in the UK called *Why I'm No Longer Talking to White People About Race* by British journalist and writer Reni Eddo-Lodge. Everyone was talking about it, even white people. The author's argument was that to constantly attempt to engage with white emotional detachment, to be constantly grappling with an audience that can't really understand is exhausting and frustrating for all parties.

I understand why she says this. But I don't want to stop talking to white people about race. I don't want to stop talking to anyone about race. I want to continue the conversations, driving them further and further into the mainstream, until there is nothing left to talk about because the violence, discrimination, and hate are all embarrassing reminders of a bygone era.

'People don't really talk about race in Singapore,' I say to Fil. Maybe what I mean is *we* don't talk about race. She shrugs as if this is something she's heard too many times before.

'There's no point,' she says, sounding uncharacteristically resigned. 'People don't listen.'

Where Do You Come From?

People like to ask me where I come from. When your skin is an unusual colour or your complexion doesn't match your accent, it can become as common as a greeting, as expected as asking about your weekend or what you had for lunch. I've developed a selection of off-the-shelf, ready-to-use answers to use depending on the situation and how I feel.

Sometimes, I reward their bluntness with the unnecessarily complex answer that is the truth. My parents are Chinese but not from China. They met as international students in Melbourne and after moving around a few years, they settled in the UK, where we've spent most of our lives. Chinese but not Chinese. British but not British. Simple.

Sometimes I just say, 'London,' which is also the truth, and that is the end of it. We move on.

In Singapore, when the question gets fired from various fronts—from a suspicious hawker auntie, a curious taxi driver, a politely sceptical colleague, confused by the erratic combination of my Asian face and home country's accent, my Chinese surname and my ang-moh husband—I have an add-on in my arsenal.

'I'm from London,' I say. 'But my mum grew up here.' I have roots. Historical links. I *belong*.

My maternal grandparents fled to Singapore after the war, their boat perhaps docking around Clifford Pier, where guests now unfurl on the outside lounge of the Fullerton Bay Hotel. Known as the 'red lamp' pier to the Chinese and Malays, the oil beacons that shine from its tip once acted as a welcome and a warning for water vehicles as they drew near

My grandparents didn't settle in Chinatown. The Shanghainese were an alien group to the predominantly Southern Chinese immigrant groups, a cliquey babble of Teochew, Hokkien, and Hakka speakers who'd laid claim to the country first. Many came later, along with the British troops who'd conceded and left the Chinese port city in 1940. They did their white neighbours' washing and tailoring. They filtered around the city—with a reputation for being shrewd businessmen, even among their fellow countrymen.

Emily, the rich girl from Ningbo, and Hai Pao, the third eldest son of a poor family, responsible for supporting his six siblings, met in the business networks of Shanghai's French concession. Russian nobles who'd fled the Bolshevik revolution had set up mansions on Chinese streets with European names.

A few metres away from the debris of the Great World entertainment centre, where on a Bloody Saturday a few years before, a bomb had exploded in front of the amusement park, which had been functioning as a makeshift refugee centre. Elsewhere in the city, Jewish fugitives seeking safety from Nazi persecution eked out a new, unfamiliar life in Hongkou. Shanghai was among the few places Jewish refugees were granted access to with no visa required.

Emily was the daughter of one of the city's most successful pawnbrokers. Hai Pao was an employee at a chemical engineering company that manufactured pharmaceuticals, working under a Japanese boss and mentor he called Sensei San, a mash-up of two honorifics to show double respect. Hai Pao was serious, hard-working, diligent with the weight of family duty, kind, and prone to the rare fit of rage. Emily was warm and sharp. She played the Chinese instrument *qin* and semi-professional volleyball. She loved Chinese calligraphy paintings, French patisserie, and sometimes, when she thought they weren't looking, would slip the best bits of her meal onto her family's plates.

Once, she told him, she had watched Japanese soldiers from her bedroom window as her frightened family had laid out fresh bed linen like a red carpet for the soldiers marching down the snow-covered street.

When the Japanese occupation ended and Mao's communist forces made their way to the city, foreign residents fled; Sensei-San disappeared. No one could tell whether he had quit or gone back to Japan, but there were new words to fill his absence. French words and English words. Bourgeois. Collaborator.

My grandparents made their own 'French exit', the quiet click of the front door while the hosts bicker over playlists and the guests sip lukewarm Chardonnay. Suddenly you've left, without any indication you're leaving, and the only mark you've left is fleeting and faded, like a quick kiss on the cheek. Hai Pao had a younger brother Harry, who had left for Singapore a few years ago and who, by all accounts, was doing quite well in the film industry. Not well enough for a spare room but well enough for a garage, which would be fine for the young couple until they found their feet.

These are the facts, the bare bones of a family history I've picked from the scraps of family conversations. There is nothing fleshier than that; my grandfather died shortly after I was born, and my grandmother passed away fifteen years later, when my teenage mind was still far too self-absorbed to want to dig into genealogy.

The story feels completely alien and unrelated to me, like it belongs to someone else and a different time, which, of course, it does. When we imagine our relatives outside the orbit of their family roles, they can sometimes feel like strangers. Maybe that is the real issue with the question 'Where do you come from?' Sometimes, even we don't really know the answer.

'I'm from London but my mum grew up here,' I squawk through my round British vowels. 'My grandparents moved here to start a new life when they were young.'

They look sceptical. Who am I trying to convince apart from myself?

Raffles

There is one place in Singapore where I feel white. The building is white, fresh plaster cast, with a milky sheen behind ornamental palm trees. The lobby is white, pillars of ashen marble between which you can have afternoon tea while a chandelier spits flecks of light onto your scones. There are lawns, manicured and croquet-ready, a wood-panelled bar furnished with rattan chairs, and a bar and billiard room under where a tiger who had escaped from a nearby circus met its fatal bullet at the turn of the twentieth century.

Raffles Hotel exudes Britishness from every polished surface, despite the fact it is managed by a French hospitality company and owned by a Qatari hotel developer. And it is named after the most famous Brit in Singapore, Sir Stamford Raffles.

Thomas Stamford Bingley Raffles is widely considered the founder of Singapore. He found it in 1819 aged thirty-seven, which by any consideration is no mean feat. I'm in my mid-thirties and finding anything further than the sock I lost behind the sofa is a pretty big deal in my book.

Raffles, pale-skinned and blue-eyed, who walked with a stoop from years of bending over badly-lit desks as a clerk in the British East India company's offices, negotiated control of the island from under the rule of usurped Malay royal Sultan Hussein Mohamed Shah and his brother, Temenggung Abdul Rahman. He bargained for the establishment of a British settlement in return for royal status in Singapore. Raffles set out to improve the island, modernize it, turn it into a British jewel of the East, a bustling free trade port, which it is still known as today.

You don't have to live in Singapore to have heard of the Raffles Hotel. It's globally renowned, at least that's what the snaking lines that spill over two flights of stairs in the hopes of getting a table at its Long Bar would indicate. Visitors come from all over the world to drink a Singapore Sling in the faux wicker chairs and eat peanuts—tossing the empty shells onto the monochrome tiled floor.

At other times, they sit on the manicured grass, reflected in the brassy metallic sheen of the Writers Bar, and drink cappuccinos or cocktails with whispery French names. They have afternoon tea under the mammoth chandelier trickling delicate crystals towards the polished marble floor. The whole building is sedately, supremely beautiful and innately *civilized*, which isn't far from what Raffles had in mind for Singapore, when he decided to colonize it.

One evening, I manage to sidle my way into a poetry reading at the Writers Bar and hear in good faith from a Raffles executive that there is a man employed to wander the property with a paintbrush and paint of the perfect shade to keep the creamy whiteness of the building continuously topped up.

If you do live in Singapore, Raffles stretches far beyond the neatly-kept grounds of the hotel. Even if he doesn't feature in everyday conversation, even if those of the younger generation claim they don't care, that—as one barista with a mullet earnestly told me—'I am more influenced by K-Pop than I am by Stamford Raffles,' he is everywhere. He is in the school textbooks and in the roads bearing names such as Stamford Road and Raffles Avenue.

'[Singapore] never really had a history worth remembering [before 1819],'[8] S. Rajaratnam, Singapore's former deputy prime minister is recorded to have said. It all started with Raffles.

It is an interesting dynamic when the course of an Asian country is swayed so heavily by the oar of one white man. Maybe that shouldn't be such an unusual concept for me. I grew up surrounded by white men in positions of power. Every local MP, almost every headteacher, every boss who has ever believed in me have all been white men. I didn't seek them out, but in a society where white male privilege was so naturally ingrained, it was a natural question of numbers and probability.

But in the case of Singapore, Raffles was the foreigner, arriving on strangers' land, planting his own ideals and ideas into its ground, his legacy turning his achievements into a conflicting tennis match of benefactor and oppressor.

Raffles opened Singapore to trade and migration, encouraging those arriving from China, India, Europe, and the Middle East to set up home in this new, free port city. He then divided the town into ethnic enclaves and established a racial hierarchy that lasted long past his legacy.

Raffles brought British concepts of law and order to the Lion City. He curbed gambling and opium smoking and introduced a system of law based on the British justice system. Many of Singapore's contemporary statutes—including those that until 2022 made homosexual relations between men illegal and the harsh capital punishment laws condemning drug carriers to death—are leftovers from the two centuries of colonial rule he kickstarted.

Raffles abolished slavery but replaced it with unforgiving decades of debt bondage. He made efforts and investments towards building a school system that would better both local children's education and teach British immigrants the local languages.

He built urban and educational infrastructure that changed local people's lives. But no matter how much he helped them advance according to prescribed western ideals, according to him, they remained inferior, almost laughable in their backwards and basic ways. The Malays he dismissed as 'so indolent that when he has rice nothing will induce him to work'. The Chinese were duplicitous, with a 'very pernicious control over the necessities of life . . . how apt they are to curry favour, how ready they are to proffer assistance when there is no danger'.[9] These were the stereotypes that lay the groundwork for a power dynamic that would last for centuries.

He did all this while only actually being present in Singapore for months on end. Most of the on-the-ground work was done by his administrator William Farquhar—a Scot with a strong sense of commercial pragmatism—and a French-Malay family, who Raffles ultimately fell out with and dismissed in 1823.

Raffles helped establish a nation, a nation proud of its governance, its resourcefulness, its people. But nation-building itself can be considered a western colonial concept, a hardening of geographical boundaries that used to be more porous done by European powers tussling for property.

That is the problem with phrases, peppered throughout western-centric histories, like 'Raffles discovered Singapore'. It erases those who had already discovered it. It blows white history up to monumental proportions, eclipsing others, those of the approximately 1,500 inhabitants living under the Malay sultanate on the 'sleepy fishing island' when Raffles arrived, whether unintentionally or on purpose.

'I think we have—for very political reasons—made Raffles a key part of Singapore's history,' says Professor Kwa Chong Guan, 'because we didn't want to focus on the Malay stories.'

Professor Kwa is a Senior Fellow at Nanyang Technological University and a Raffles expert. He wrote some of the school textbooks teaching future generations of Singaporeans about him. He co-wrote a textbook published in 2009 to be taught in secondary schools called *Singapore: A 700-year History*, which goes beyond the 1819 starting line and explores recent archaeological evidence of a fourteenth century emporium on the main island. Singapore, the book argues, was a trading port and a thriving commercial hub under the Malaccan Sultanate before Raffles even arrived.

In the first years of Singapore's post-war years, a towering statue of Raffles was reinstated from its wartime hiding place in a museum. It remained, even after independence, as a symbol that the country was open to international trade and still held its crown as an 'emporium of the East'.

For Singapore's bicentennial, Singaporean artist Teng Kai Wei took part in a collaboration to make a polymarble copy of the original bronze statue on Boat Quay, creating an optical illusion that seemed to make Raffles fade into the background of high-rises behind him. He was also joined by four statue neighbours, which sprang up overnight: Sang Nila Utama of the mistaken lion sighting; Munshi Abdullah, Raffles' secretary and Malay tutor, widely regarded as the founder of modern Malay literature; Tan Tock Seng, Chinese-Singaporean philanthropist and community leader; and Naraina Pillai, Tamil social entrepreneur and businessman.

The piece was a nod to the multicultural, multi-ethnic Singaporeans who also helped develop the city-state. But what about the thousands of other forgotten, nameless people that had helped build the country and the statues themselves?

ASSEMBLING A PERSONAL HISTORY

Crazy Rich Asians

I saw Singapore before I really saw Singapore. I saw it through a lens of glossy montages, luxury fashion, and beautiful people speaking in cut-glass international school accents against a soundtrack of jazzed up fifties Chinese pop and Mandarin covers of Coldplay. We didn't need to buy a plane ticket. Everyone else had seen it too. There was a new ethnicity-based question du jour and it was not 'Where do you come from?'

It was, 'Have you seen *Crazy Rich Asians*?'

Of course I had seen *Crazy Rich Asians*, the 2018 blockbuster romantic comedy following Chinese-American Rachel as she follows her boyfriend Nick back home and into the complex social labyrinth of Singapore's mega-wealthy. I devoured it the way I had gobbled *Joy Luck Club* twenty-five years before, a nineties child lapping up the film version of Amy Tan's Asian American 1989 hit exploring love, rivalry, and how to pass down intergenerational trauma through cooked crab.

It didn't matter that the *Joy Luck Club* gang had bouffant hairstyles and yuppy neuroses while I was eight and played with Pokémon, just as, two decades later, it didn't matter that Rachel had a New York accent and an PhD in Economics. These were some of the only movies starring characters who looked a bit like me. These were my people!

Then, we relocated to Singapore. And now, I am finding that my preconception of the movie as the written gospel on the Southeast Asian experience has been firmly crushed, like an unwelcome cockroach scuttling across a shiny new high-rise.

* * *

I am in Lauren's apartment, a cosy immaculate one-bedroom in Katong. It is our first Thanksgiving in Singapore. Our first Thanksgiving ever.

The gang around Lauren's neat table are almost all internationally educated Malaysian Chinese or Singaporean Chinese. They're real 'citizens of the world', making wry observations about racist microaggressions at European boarding schools or how a Singaporean colleague tried to teach them how to eat chicken rice ('They asked me if I knew how to dip the chicken in the sauces! Like my mum doesn't make the best chicken rice in California'). They've imported Thanksgiving from years at various Ivy League universities.

And now, as the turkey is sliced open, we are dissecting *Crazy Rich Asians*.

'Wye Mun is one of the worst representations of an Asian dad I've ever seen,' starts Mel. Gentle, funny, razor-sharp smart Mel is my first friend in Singapore. She moved to the Lion City after growing up in Hong Kong and boarding schools in the States. I met her through my friend in London, Kim, who took pity on me arriving friendless in a new country and hooked me up with her old school friend from Hong Kong. For anyone moving to a new country, I highly recommend this method of making new friends (the slow spread of networks from trusted buddies that is. Not pity).

The rest of the table chip in with their own attacks.

Why are they driving in an open-air Jeep? No one would do that unless they're in the armed forces. No real Singaporean sounds like Peik Lin or her family. Why are they making dumplings? That is a northern Chinese thing, not a Southeast Asian southern Chinese immigrant thing.

Where are the other ethnic races in this multiracial country?

What is with the lack of Singlish?!

Later, over carrots glazed in a sticky maple polish, it is conceded that the matriarch grandmother's family is originally from Beijing, so the dumpling-making scene is not as heinously inaccurate as we first thought. Still, the verdict has been drawn. *Crazy Rich Asians* is a gilded illusion. Its Singapore is not our Singapore. This is the trouble with representation that has been filtered through the lens of Hollywood, concerned with the appeal to 'mainstream', western audiences. The problem with representation is that it's so sparse, one movie becomes burdened with representing an entire country or culture.

The film is based on Singaporean author Kevin Kwan's book of the same name. Kwan, a descendent of one of the country's oldest banking families, is the epitome of 'crazy rich Asian' generational wealth.

When his family relocated to Texas, then eleven-year-old Kevin was hit by a culture shock. He swapped high-end Singapore for suburban American lawn-mowing. He missed 'not having ten things for breakfast'. He started documenting his experiences like a curious anthropologist, both insider and outsider to an elusive section of Singaporean society.

His memories fuelled his stories, and for as many complaints I find about *Crazy Rich Asians* on the internet and at Thanksgiving parties, there are also some saying that they know people like this and their lifestyles, that they've rubbed shoulders with them in the Lion City.

There are nuances in the book the film has airbrushed. Kwan's dialogue is peppered with Singlish. There is the pristine exclusiveness of Sentosa Cove. The snobbery against mainland Chinese. A country of immigrants fighting ravenously for their fortunes. Phrases and idiosyncrasies toned down in the film to make the story more 'accessible'.

Kwan's book did not set out to represent an entire ethnic or cultural experience. It is a fantastical, fun portrayal of a small section of East and Southeast Asian society, tinged by Kwan's own personal story as part of the elite 1 per cent. But it also tackles themes that are both colour-blind and universal: love, friendship, family politics, feeling both too much and not enough. It's a story that 'transcends race', Kwan said in an interview, after revealing his favourite reaction to the movie was hearing 'two white dudes' in Philadelphia admitting it had moved them to tears.

Kwan has also spoken about the pressure when deciding to release it as a film, the fear that 'if this movie bombs, there will never be another Asian movie done for fifty years'. There were the nervous questions from Hollywood about accessibility. Would non-Asians be interested in watching a film so heavily immersed in an Asian family's dynamics and dysfunctions?

Another reason *Crazy Rich Asians* stayed in the headlines was that a year after its release, lead actress Constance Wu succumbed to the ultimate symptom of superstar fame. She got cancelled.

Wu was one of the stars in *Fresh off the Boat*, another diaspora comedy where she starred as that well-trodden stereotype, the Asian tiger mum. After the comedy was commissioned for a sixth series by the American TV network ABC, the Virginia-born star released a series of tweets showing she was less than enthusiastic about the news. 'So upset right now that I'm literally crying. Ugh,' ran her online rant. When one user congratulated her on the good news, she replied, 'No it's not.'[10] Soon, the online stratosphere condemned her as a 'blight on the Asian American community'.[11] In her memoir *Making a Scene*, Wu spoke about the feeling that 'if I was so lucky as to be on that playing field . . . I had to be perfect and gracious . . . or else they'd never let anyone else on'. This speaks to the fear and accountability of carrying an entire ethnicity, to be 'all Asians' just by virtue of being Asian.

Pressure plays a starring role in the story of representation. Would more stories from diverse and different backgrounds and countries allow the space for Asian actors and writers to be themselves without the weight of being everyone else from their country or their continent?

There's been a slow influx of East and Southeast Asian stories in international media over the past few years, like *Past Lives*, *Joy Ride*, *Beef*. The team behind *Crazy Rich Asians* has announced that a sequel is unlikely.[12] There is still a focus on the large-eyed, fairer-skinned, American East Asian diaspora, but the global success of Korean film *Parasite* and series *Squid Game* has shown a new direction for these so-called 'minority trailblazers' on the international landscape.

In the meantime, I walk past the powder-blue Tan Kim Seng Fountain with its stucco white muses and cupids, across the jagged steps at Esplanade Park, where slabs of concrete are stacked like Jenga blocks as they creep out towards the waterfront. This was the location of one of the climactic scenes in *Crazy Rich Asians*. The movie version is glossier, but it is still pretty impressive in real life. The lights from the buildings and from the bridge lamps across the harbour toss shards of multicoloured light across the water.

Does it matter if we polish reality for the shine of the silver screen? If the result is a wider awareness and representation of different cultures because we choose the most enticing stories and make them more relatable at the cost of accuracy, do the ends justify the means? I don't have the philosophical nous or the Hollywood mega-bucks to give a definitive answer.

But I'm thinking of a line in Kwan's book that—intentionally or not—made me a bit sad. Nick is telling Rachel about the last, somewhat forgotten indigenous Malay king with whom Raffles bargained control over the island for a royal status in Singapore. A different kind of Rich Asian. Rachel, liking the sound of 'The Last King of Singapore', suggests it would make a good movie. Nick is dismissive.

'I think it would draw an audience of about four people,' he says.

Going to the Movies

I watch Southeast Asian movies. I visit The Projector, a sharp indie cinema inside a stark Brutalist building with soft, rounded edges where I watched *La Luna*, a romantic comedy about a city girl who shakes up the suffocating traditions of a sleepy Malay village by opening a lingerie shop. The director M. Raihan Halim's most recent film *Ibu* was a horror story about a mother who risks losing her stepdaughter to a *pontianak*, the ghost of a woman who died in childbirth.

The Projector's white bar gives off a dull light like the billboards of old movie theatres. I strike up a conversation with a young film producer sitting on one of its battered sofas.

'Horror stories are popular in Southeast Asian, especially Malay, films because they're easy to make allegories from, to comment on social issues,' she tells me. 'Plus, our folklore is full of ghosts.'

I watch *Ah Boys to Men*, a cult classic comedy romp through National Service in Singapore that feels like Kevin and Perry in camouflage. I feast on the artsy and the silly. There is no snobbery in this cultural critic.

Then, one day, in the Cathay Gallery—a private gallery dedicated to the biggest film empire in Southeast Asia, where monochrome reels play Hong Kong romcoms and Malaysian horror movies, and where rows of folded seats and memorabilia remind us that outside the shining lights of Hollywood, Southeast Asia has been running its own thriving film industry for decades—I see someone who looks like me. Not in the same way I hope, over-optimistically, that actors like Constance Wu or Katie Leung look a bit like me. This man, with his square jaw and serious eyes framed by square-rimmed glasses, looks a bit like me because we come from the same pool of DNA.

My great-uncle Harry. The missing brother of my grandfather Hai Pao. I've found him, printed in monochrome, stuck to the walls of a private museum, watching me like a phantom from family stories or a character from a movie you've never seen but feel like you know.

Harry Chow

Harry Chow moved to the Lion City from China, where he'd played the harmonica for Radio Shanghai. He came to work in movies and arrived at just the right time.

Singapore was searching for a new post-war, post Japanese-occupation identity and they found it on the silver screen. The fifties blossomed as a golden era of regional film. Movies were shot and produced locally and watched in indoor and outdoor cinemas. At midnight on 27 April 1957, the original *Pontianak* film sparked an unexpected craze for Malay horror films.

The company behind *Pontianak* was Cathay, and the man behind Cathay was Loke Wan Tho. Loke was a businessman, ornithologist, and photographer, who carried an anthology of poetry in his personal kit whenever he travelled. He was also Harry's boss, and on one June evening, the two were in Taiwan to brave the glitz and glamour of the 1964 Asian Film Festival in Taipei.

Like his booking manager Harry, Loke was drawn to the bright lights and rough and tumble of the movie industry. His own life had played out as a series of dramatic vignettes of triumph over adversity. He was a frail, sickly young boy who had flourished into an athletics champion at a Swiss boarding school. The ship he was on was bombed and sunk as he tried to flee to Indonesia during World War II as a young man. He was rescued by an Australian cruiser and made a full recovery from burns and partial blindness in an Indian hospital.[13]

He took over the family film business after the Japanese surrender, and, by the end of the forties, expanded his empire through Penang, Borneo, and Thailand to become one of the wealthiest men in Singapore. The symbol of his success towered over the city in the Cathay building, a former Japanese broadcast and propaganda centre, the entrance to which they had flanked with the severed heads of those who'd stepped out of line. It was now a sixteen-storey air-conditioned art deco cultural hub where you could watch exotic foreign films in technicolour.

Sometimes, Harry's own life also seemed like it had been stolen from a movie. There were private views and parties with people who yelled 'Cut!' and 'Action!' not just over films but over countries. Harry's son John had a framed picture in his room next to Hayley Mills who had just finished shooting *Pollyanna.* Once, during an evening where suited executives slunk around regional actresses like sharks, a man introduced himself to Harry. It was Roy Disney.

Harry helped his brother, Hai Pao set up a small business selling film production equipment, with Cathay as their major client. When Hai Pao and Emily, my grandparents, eventually swapped the garage they were camping out in for a small, terraced house off MacPherson, the two brothers would meet on Sundays and amble in friendly silence around the water's edge to the imposing stone columns of the general post office to pick up deliveries. A pause between takes. A deep, fresh breath of reality. Family time.

But that was then. By 1964, the political disturbances in the city-state and failing investments rubbed off some of Cathay's stardust. Fear of local gangsterism and western fads was causing a government crackdown on open-air cinema gatherings and a ban on 'unsuitable' content. Three years ago, there had been a sit-down protest of cinema workers outside Cathay-Keris's studio demanding higher wages and better working conditions. Loke was troubled.

To make matters worse, things were not going well at the Taipei film festival. Two of his leading stars had been nominated for mere supporting role awards. The closing ceremony was drawing near, and Loke needed a distraction. He'd heard of a museum in Taichung, a thirty-minute flight from Taipei, with impressive porcelain exhibits. Just what he needed. He organized a private plane and rallied a group of colleagues, including Harry and his wife Milly.

Our lives are a projector's reel of scenes, both mundane and pivotal. We keep playing different parts for different people; and, after we're gone, we're rewatched on the screens of memories, moulded to fit someone else's narrative or immortalized in the pages, paragraphs, or footnotes of the period.

That is where the story of my great-uncle Harry stops. Whether it is over a rare cousins' get-together, where it emerges after a third drink, or in monochrome displays across museum walls, this is where it ends. He died in the B-908 plane crash that killed Loke Wan Tho and the fifty-six other passengers and crew onboard.

It's been glamorously recorded in Singaporean cinematic history as 'the end of an era'.

My Uncle John

My uncle John remembers his father's harmonica music. The jangled notes like piecemeal memories from when he used to play the instrument for Radio Shanghai. Their house was on Emerald Hill, a terracotta-coloured shophouse with dark wooden shutters. It was haunted. When the dusk light streamed through the shutters' slats, John would see a dismembered hand inching its way across the landing towards his bedroom.

'It was a hand from the war,' he says simply. 'The Japanese would cut off the limbs of prisoners. Some of the separated body parts decided to hang around.'

There are other things he remembers. The rhythmic tapping of the typewriter keys when his mother worked. The gifts his father would bring back from his business trips—a brass trumpet, a Chinese violin with snakeskin, because he knew his son loved music.

There was a small funeral at their house after the plane crash, and my mum got the porcelain doll she had always wanted, an almost spotless leftover picked up from the damp luggage.

* * *

There are other things my uncle John has kept, not just in his memories, but in the dimly-lit study where bright model airplanes dangle like coloured hangmen from the ceiling. He hands one to me when he and Aunt Elsie are paying a fleeting visit to his home country in between updates from his childhood haunts. The Fullerton Hotel is where his father and my grandfather used to go to collect their mail every day, back when the ridged stone columns housed the post office. His childhood house on Emerald Hill is now a trendy tapas bar. The pavements of Beach Road where he used to fish with his father are now full of restaurants where we take him to eat fluffy mounds of coconut rice and crispy ayam goreng, at a trendy tropical café that spills onto the sidewalk where sand used to kiss the sea.

Over the pillow of sunny egg-stained rice, he pushes a plastic bag towards me, one that is straining at the seams like it has had a really good summer holiday. My uncle John can't walk through a protest without taking a pamphlet, so this is not a huge surprise. Except these papers are from sixty years ago. There are newspaper clippings, evidence folders, investigation reports. They are neatly bound and gagged in caramel-coloured cardboard with thick masking tape.

They describe the pillar of smoke rising from a nearby paddy field and the charred designer handbags around the bodies.

There is a conspiracy theory, which he clings onto like the selfie stick he has taken to carrying everywhere to 'document our family history'. Two of the muddy corpses had purported links to the Taiwanese military. They had allegedly planned to defect to communist Beijing. The Civil Air Transport, the Chinese Nationalist Airline that owned the plane, had been acquired by the Central Intelligence Agency (CIA) in 1950. The American intelligence agency took part in an investigation but couldn't make any definitive conclusion on the cause of the crash. Later, an American Civil Air Transport pilot released a tell-all memoir. The chapter dedicated to the crash is short and the words are blunt and straightforward. 'We got hijacked,' it says. 'It was a cunning plan for the Communists . . . Loke Wan Tho . . . had donated hefty sums of money to the Nationalist government.'

* * *

We hang onto things after people die. Mementoes, memories, the comfort of conspiracy theories. But most of all we hang onto questions. What if? Why? We join our loved ones underground, looking for answers, which give us closure and keep us close.

My uncle John has a photo. In it, his father Harry is standing with his arms around Chinese revolutionary and former Nationalist president Chiang Kai-shek, who spent the later years of his life in exile in Taiwan, at loggerheads with Mao's increasingly powerful communist regime. 'Did you know your grandmother had all her assets and valuable possessions confiscated when the red guards raided her family's home in Ningbo before she left for Singapore to start a new life?' Uncle John asks me.

My grandmother never mentioned this.

Soon after the plane crash, John was shipped to a Jesuit boarding school in Melbourne. Australia was a sunny land of opportunity and the occasional kangaroo. A good place, the family thought, to start again.

'The Jesuits were really strict,' he remembers. 'And the other kids were just confused. I was the first Asian kid they'd seen, and because of the war, they just assumed I was Japanese.'

The headlines stopped printing stories about the mysterious Cathay crash years ago. My uncle John's letter to the Golden Horse Film Festival asking if he could visit the site of the crash went unanswered. Even at family dinners, it is rarely mentioned, relegated to the back shelves of family folklore, waiting for the next generation to unearth and briefly return to the spotlight.

How to Be a Woman

Singapore is a pretty good place to be a woman. It is one of the safest countries in the world. The round surveillance cameras taped to lampposts in rundown areas remind us that there are higher powers looking out for us.

Singapore is a pretty good place to be a woman. It has one of the highest percentage of CEO roles held by women in the world and a steadily growing number of female board members.[14] You can freeze your eggs until the age of thirty-seven. You can join the forces (but unlike the men, you don't *have* to). You live in a country that has one of the smallest gender parity gaps in Southeast Asia, second only to the Philippines.[15]

The boundless opportunities of a modern Singaporean woman are demonstrated in an Instagram video by the insurance company AIA to mark 2023's International Women's Day.[16] The stars of this post are a happy pink-faced, blob-eared cartoon family, but the *real* star is the superhero mum.

'She's a boss!' exclaims a caption as she clacks furiously on an Apple laptop.

'She's also a really great chef!' as she nods over a plump roast chicken.

'And also my homework checker!' as she sits at a table decked in a T-shirt marked 'Educator'.

This perky two-dimensional woman is a superhero.

It looks exhausting.

I meet women outside the cartoon dimension in Singapore. Cheerful, laid-back Yasmine who juggles a career in corporate events with the role of a 'good Muslim wife', looking after her husband and six children. Tina, who settled in Singapore with her Australian husband to escape the cultural pressures and baffled disappointment of her family back home in the Philippines at her choice to remain child-free.

I learn that there isn't really a definition of what it means to be a woman in Singapore, just as there isn't really a definition for what it means to woman in the UK, or anywhere else. I ask this to my friend Lauren, a Swiss-educated Singaporean, free-spirited entrepreneur, adventurous homebody who lives ten minutes from her childhood home in Katong, a flat she's in only a few days a month as she travels the globe for work.

'When I think about women in Singapore today, the biggest thing that comes to mind is contradiction,' she says.

Singapore is a pretty good place to be a woman because of the relative bounty of opportunities. But this bounty creates a banquet of frantically spinning plates heaped with pressure. It creates a squeezed generation of women providing care to both younger and older generations, corseted by cultural expectations of motherhood and filial piety, and the pressure to be a career woman, because that is what a modern young progressive country needs, but also start a family, because that is what traditional Asian values still expect. Become a mother and you receive a slew of government bonuses, but less so if you are a single mother, who won't be eligible for the 2023 budget's enhanced baby bonus cash gifts.

Singapore can be a pretty good place to be a woman, but like the tall, somewhat phallic high-rises, pointing their tips towards the smoggy clouds in the central business district, the glitzy promise of progress obscures the fact that it hasn't always been this way. And that there is still so much more to be done.

Lessons from My Mother

We learn how to be a woman from a variety of sources. We learn it from the cultures we are raised in, the expectations sculpted from centuries of gender norms. We learn it from the television and magazines and novels; we learn it from books by authors such as Caitlin Moran, who has written a book literally titled *How to Be a Woman*. We learn it from our girl friends and our guy friends, our partners and our children. But before all that, we learn it from our mothers.

We're shaped by the umbilical cord that ties us together in the womb, passing on a squishy mix of nutrients, love, and anxiety. We learn it from the way she brushed our hair, the way she talked us through our first period, the way we see her act around men, women, friends, colleagues. We're moulded by her presence, its soft comfort and biting rage, and if we never had or have lost a mother figure, we're moulded by her absence too.

Here are some things I learned from my mother:

1. You can always judge a man by his quality and choice of shoes.
2. Some moisturizers can double up as a sneaky make-up remover if you're strapped on cash and time.
3. There are always options. Some may not seem like the best options, but they're almost always better than feeling trapped.
4. Never be friends with someone who is rude to waiters.
5. Friendships aren't always going to last forever, but that makes the ones that last more important.
6. You can't trust anyone more than your partner.
7. But no one will trust you more than your dog.
8. People are more likely to be thinking about their own lives than judging yours.

9. If you're going to do something, do it properly.
10. Never compromise on the big things: food, home, family.
11. And above all, always remember you will need to work twice as hard to get just as far as everyone else. Once because you're Asian. Once because you are a woman.

I remember her saying this on the school run through west London terraced houses and in the sleepy suburban streets in Melbourne, her red lipstick put on like warrior paint. I remember my fierce ambition to prove myself when I was in primary school, to always be the 'best' by standards set by others. I remember the sour fear in my stomach throughout my teens and early twenties, the belief that I was only a sum of my productivity, of other people's approval, that I was always functioning two steps behind.

My mother taught us to be fighters—us against the world. She taught us to make it our default setting. Did she learn this from her mother as a bubbly, frizzy-haired kid at the dawn of Singapore's independence? What wisdom did my grandmother pass down that helped her become a woman?

Things My Mother Learned from Her Mother

From her mother, my mother learned the joy of a brushstroke, the way that the darkness of your words on paper can stain deeper than a thousand spoken words. She learned the light, frivolous balm of eating something sweet to soothe sadness, and why both sadness and sweet things are sometimes best shared.

She learned the right things and some wrong things. She learned to believe she would never quite belong, even in a country where most people looked like her. The ethnic majority but not the majority, the fuzzy Vs and Zs of her parents' Shanghainese drowned out by clipped Cantonese consonants. Both insider and outsider.

She learned to always judge herself by other people's standards, that appearances are everything—the lessons of a young country forming its own identity, a ravenous meritocracy looking for benchmarks to measure social worth.

She learned that presents were business transactions, and that everything had a price. The shiny new doll given to my mum by a family acquaintance sat untouched on the top shelf of a cupboard until it could be gifted to the child of another business colleague, passed on like a favour.

She learned that saving money was good, but saving face was better. She learned that the most important thing is family—your successes are my success, and your failures are my failures. She watched my grandmother stack the shelves with pyramids of colourful cans, drums of condensed milk as, outside, the 1964 rioters grabbed bottles and poles to smash buildings and skulls, and she learned the meaning of 'bunker mentality': hope for the best but prepare for the worst.

She learned that once someone has lived through war, a part of them always remains there. Even years later in Singapore, there would always be a corner of my grandmother's mind that heard the sound of Japanese boots crunching a scar through a snow-covered Shanghainese street.

My mother felt the sharp whip of the cane across her shins and heard the angry arguments between her parents, hissed shouts full of loneliness and regret and homesickness for a life that didn't exist anymore. She learned anger was unbecoming for a woman but sometimes you need anger to survive, to power through each day, each new opportunity. She learned that there were always options, that when one door shuts, you can prise another open, but it may not stay open for long.

My mother learned that home isn't a fixed location. That family and identity are things that you carry with you like suitcases and souvenirs.

She inherited a restlessness, a feeling that the world was out there waiting and that her forever home was just one move away. That you never know what the next move might bring. The family had left Singapore by the time my mother was fifteen, drawn by the prospect of western schooling for their children in Melbourne. Education is everything—that is another lesson my mother learned.

She learned other things too, not from her mother—how to speak in a blended international accent to fit in; that cheap port at a student night is a mistake; that she hated ABBA and liked Tracy Chapman's 'Fast Car'.

I think about my mother and grandmother every time I try something new or a friend calls me brave. I see them in my ease with strangers, the way I've learned to adapt fast to new situations. I see them too in my impatience, my flightiness, the way I jump to conclusions. Like them, I'm quick to love and quick to hurt.

These are the things we learn from our mothers—lessons, quirks, insecurities, passed down like strands of DNA.

Things passed down from my grandmother to my mother to me, three generations of daughters. Innate. Absorbed. Inherited. They're lessons you don't need to teach.

(MOTHER)LAND

Sex Miseducation

The first thing I learned about sex was how to put a condom on a banana.

It was in a science classroom when we were twelve years old. We'd been waiting for this. Nothing travels faster through a class of gawky pre-teens than news of their first sex education class. The news spread more speedily than herpes (which wasn't on the curriculum until the next term anyway).

The fate of your future sexual prowess was set on those lab benches by a giggly jury. If you struggled to suffocate your banana or, even worse, broke it, you were destined for a life of giving bad hand jobs. Rumours said that if bananas weren't in stock at the local supermarket then we would be forced to spend an hour slipping a greasy Durex over whatever was available. An aubergine perhaps. Or an avocado. The levels of teenage angst varied, but the underlying message was constant.

'You are modern progressive women of the future. You have your whole lives ahead of you. The one way to really mess it all up now, is to get pregnant.'

This warning was hammered into our bones and libidos throughout our teenage years. Then suddenly, around our thirtieth birthday, the narrative flipped completely, disconcertingly, on its head. At some point, the ideal of a responsible woman swerves from carefully child-free to child-focused, prepping for the all-important role of a mother before you run out of time.

I went to an all-girls school in South England. I've heard sex education has become slightly more enlightened since the early noughties. There are Netflix series on the subject now. But the after-effects of this conditioning and its sudden U-turn have hit my generation like whiplash. I've heard its reverberations through podcasts, interviews, friends' anecdotes. I've heard it in the frustrated monologue of British actress Gemma Chan as her character fumes against societal expectations in the Channel 4 mini-film *I Am Hannah*.

'We've been told from our teenage years to our twenties . . . the worst thing that can happen is to get pregnant. It's drilled into us from such a young age, and then suddenly it switches. It goes from, don't get pregnant to you'd better fucking get pregnant or you've missed your chance. That change happens in five years and it's . . . just like, "What the fuck?"'

M/Other

Fast forward a couple of decades. I am in a small dessert bar in Holland Village, a smart residential suburb where my own mum spent her Singaporean childhood. The room is full of women. A glossy-haired artist speaks to a small crowd about her adoption journey. A Filipino domestic worker shares how her heart and commitment are torn between two countries and two little boys, her expat charge and her youngest son back home. Over cubes of sticky date cake, I strike up conversation with a shy woman with stunning sleeve tattoos. She tells me how she gave birth to her son nine months after a violent rape attack.

We are not here for dessert. We are here to celebrate the book that lies in multiple copies across the tables. The book which features these women and the thing that brings them together. It is on the front cover in bold white letters against a rainbow background: 'M/Other'. We are here to celebrate Otherness. We are here to celebrate Motherhood.

'I wanted to provide a platform, for male and female alike, who typically may not have the agency to tell their story,' *M/Other*'s author Loretta Chen tells me later.

Loretta is a multi-hyphenate: an AI entrepreneur, author, academic, and an outsider committed to giving others outside the trammels of social norms a voice. *M/Other* features interviews with foster parents, same-sex parents, survivors of sexual assault, each sharing their stories of parenthood outside Singapore's conventional norms.

'I think it's interesting that even though we're one of the richest countries in the world, one of the most highly educated countries in the world, one of the most air-conditioned . . . for all intents and purposes, we are still incredibly Confucian,' she muses.

Traditional Confucian values entail the Asian philosophy that puts family at the core of moral and social well-being. But we can't put it all on Confucius. He advocated for 'big families and small government',[17] and this seems almost the opposite of what Singapore is going through—declining birth-rates and proactive input from the state towards family planning.

Single, unwed, foreign, divorced, widowed parents are eligible for certain grants and tax rebates. Monthly stipends of $300–$600 are offered to help working single parents with infant and childcare, as well as other forms of aid. But overall single mothers (and it is still overwhelmingly the mothers who take on the childcare in many of these dynamics) face longer waiting times for government housing, shorter household childcare leave, and less financial assistance than those in conventional heteronormative partnerships.

It is not a question of money. Minister for Social and Family Development Masagos Zulkifli stated it himself in a May 2023 Prime Minister's Questions: 'It is not an issue of costs . . . but that each of these policies reflect prevailing societal norms and values, that of parenthood within marriage.'[18]

However, it goes deeper than that and is embedded in the mentality that spurred 60 per cent of Singaporeans in a 2019 survey to admit they feel parenthood out of wedlock was unacceptable.[19] This was the mentality Zulkifli fuelled when he stressed the difference between 'support' and 'incentive', upon being challenged on whether single parents should be included in the baby bonus, after being told that the median employment income for single mothers under thirty-five is around $700 a month.[20]

'Creating an environment of greater empathy . . . for single unwed parents to raise their children requires a whole-of-society effort,' said the minister in 2021.[21] And he is right. But society flows from those at the top. As is evident in the establishment of the Singapore Family Planning Association in 1949 to provide contraceptive services and regulate the population in a stretched post-war nation; the 'Stop at Two' campaign of the seventies; and the Social Development Unit of the eighties, a glorified government dating service, which arranged events to match-make accomplished Singaporean singles. It was launched to tackle the issue of highly-educated women remaining unmarried and continues under the rebranded name Social Development Network today.

'We are not divorced from our personal backgrounds,' says Loretta firmly. 'We are not divorced from the views we have about the world. Of course the personal is political.'

* * *

Singapore is a good place to start a family. I was told this a whole four days after I arrived, by a pretty bird-like fashion designer, who touched my arm as she said it with a conspiratorial wink. Education standards are among the world's best here, and childcare is accessible.

But Singapore can be a good place to not start a family too. Abortion is legal, unlike some Southeast Asian countries, and has been since 1970. But this autonomy is arguably backed by a wider message that it is the right sort of families that are welcome, that certain people should make the cut to parenthood, according to Loretta.

'We want to seem very progressive,' observes Loretta. 'But the covert undertone is that we just uphold heteronormativity. If falling birth rates are the issue, why can't we make adoption policies easier? Why can't we make fostering policies easier?'

Loretta wrote her book during the pit of the pandemic. Mothers, juggling increasingly precarious jobs with family demands, were among the hardest hit. During the height of the health crisis, Loretta's mother suffered a stroke. She recovered, but Loretta, shut in her current home country of Hawaii, spent many terrified moments thinking she'd seen her own mother for the last time. *M/Other* is dedicated to her.

'She was born in 1938, and when I was growing up in the eighties, women were still expected to be fairly conservative,' Loretta remembers. 'But she would speak up. She didn't cower. And she would always defend me.'

It was Loretta's mother who taught her to ignore gender norms and religious divisions. She took her to temples of various faiths and walked past the signs warning that womanhood and menstruation were dirty.

She supported her daughter's bisexuality and her decision to not have children. 'I don't think she thought she was being a feminist,' Loretta muses. 'But I think because she never gave me a sense of shame, I am who I am now. And I'm so grateful for how she's raised me.'

In *M/Other*'s preface, Loretta describes her truth observing motherhood from the outside. 'Motherhood in whatever configuration is not easy. It can be a painful, frustrating, soul-consuming, thankless task. It can also be an enriching, rewarding, and joyous experience that I am told is peerless.'

A love like that is terrifying. Love and fear. Those are the common bonds that Loretta found tied together all the unconventional mothers in her project. Love and fear, those two vital ingredients of what it means to be a parent. Perhaps, what it means to be human.

A National Birthday

There are two balloons in the shop window, gold and buoyant with happy helium. They are in the shape of chubby numbers, five and seven. There are banners stretched across windows shouting 'Happy fifty-seventh birthday!' A bar is offering a happy hour special, but only for those who have hit the three quarter mark on their fifth decade.

Someone is turning fifty-seven. We are all turning fifty-seven. Singapore is turning fifty-seven. It is National Day.

National Day begins weeks before the actual National Day on 9 August. It starts when shops start selling merchandise and the roads close so rehearsals for the annual parade can take place.

There are rumours it never rains on National Day. They say weeks before, a specially formed weather monitoring taskforce seeds the clouds, shooting tiny spurs of ice into their fluffy bodies so the downpour comes early. The whole thing is organized with a stereotypically Singaporean efficiency, thoroughness, and nerve-gnawing fear of something going wrong.

These stories of cloud-seeding for special occasions persist like urban fables, spreading like grumbling storm clouds despite then-Minister for the Environment and Water Resources Vivian Balakrishnan refuting them almost ten years ago in 2015.

I buy a bunch of red and white flags, the thin crescent moon of a young nation rising, among five stars for each Singaporean value: justice, equality, democracy, peace, and progress.

I invite Mel and Lauren over and we watch the fireworks wearing red and white party hats. We play a card game called 'The Singaporean Dream', a crazy mix of Monopoly and Pokémon, where each player takes on an identity of a particular national stereotype. Mel is a brand-ravenous influencer; Paul is the auntie; Lauren is the ambitious CEO; and I am a dedicated young military serviceman. We bargain, negotiate, and fight for cards tailored to our own special Singaporean dream: a promotion for the CEO, wedding sponsorship for the influencer. The whole thing is silly, fun, and definitely helped by the fizzy bottle of prosecco we have bought to add a festive feel.

As we are sipping bubbles, Mel announces that she is applying for Singaporean citizenship. 'The way things are developing with China back home at the moment, it's hard for me to feel like I belong there,' she says simply. 'I don't know if I feel Singaporean, but I definitely don't feel from Hong Kong anymore.'

Citizenship is a holy grail for the expats who've settled in Singapore, who've dug roots into the country's tropical soil so deep they can't imagine leaving. Singapore grants up to around 22,000 new citizenship requests each year, including automatic passport rights for children born to Singaporean parents abroad. Around 23,500 new citizenships were granted in 2023.[22]

What does it mean to belong to a country? For hopeful prospective Singaporeans, before they get their citizenship officially approved, it involves a three-pronged process: an e-learning webinar, a visit to key historical landmarks, and a community sharing session. This final stage focuses on three parts: past, present, and future. How did you integrate as a new arrival to Singapore? How do you fit into your community? What are your visions for our country, and what will you bring to the table?

This year's annual National Day song is headed by local spiky-haired and baby-faced crooner and Singapore Idol winner, Taufik Batisah. It's called 'Stronger Together', and it is a gum-festeringly sweet pop melody set against a video montage of sunset-streaked waterfronts and inspiring Singaporean stories and romantic black-and-white photographs. The saccharine chords are stuck in my head for weeks.

The first National Day wasn't much cause for celebration. For Singapore's first prime minister Lee Kuan Yew, who had fought for a united alliance with the Malayan states and led the country through two uneasy years of merger with Malaysia, independence meant failure.

'I was close to physical exhaustion. I was weighed down by a heavy sense of guilt,' he recalls in his memoir, *The Singapore Story*. 'I felt I had let down several million people in Malaysia: immigrant Chinese and Indians, Eurasians and . . . some Malays. I had aroused their hopes and they had joined people in Singapore in resisting Malay hegemony, the root cause of our dispute. I was ashamed that I had left our allies and supporters to fend for themselves.'

When Lee describes the first few years of building a nation from scratch in 'a tough world of nationalistic new states in Southeast Asia', it is with caution and reminders of 'how we nearly did not make it'.

I wonder what these fearful ghosts do for patriotism. Countries tend to mark milestones of historical pride: the storming of the Bastille, the Declaration of Independence. Here, we are celebrating an independence we had foisted upon us. We are honouring a feeling of 'this wasn't what we planned for but look how far we've come with it'.

In Singapore and Singaporeans, I see an understated sense of everyday patriotism, a quiet pride in a country that had independence thrust upon it. It is in the tote bags you see lining up in the supermarket queues, imprinted with the logos for SG 50, the Lion City's half century birthday almost a decade ago. It is in the rows of bunting flanking the windows of the HDB apartments. It is in the words of Patricia Chan, Singapore's 'Golden Girl' of swimming, who led the country to victory in its first Southeast Asian Peninsular Games. 'Young though we may have been . . . it was quite clear there was a new flag to represent . . . new colours to fly, and . . . a sense of well, look, this is what we can do,' she said in a CNA interview.[23]

The flags are taken down by the end of September. National Day is done and dusted. Singaporeans are done with celebrating their country and are moving forward, working to keep their country going, make it something to be proud of, a nation worth celebrating.

For My Country

Something happens to a Singaporean man when he turns eighteen. He gets married. Every fit, young, red-blooded male Singaporean is technically taken. It might seem hasty, but if you saw his partner, you really couldn't blame him. Her toned body, her protective nature. Her comforting weight resting against his shoulder. Her sleek grooved barrel and unbeatable accuracy at firing long-range bullets.

Something happens to a Singaporean man when he turns eighteen. He is taken to a base on Pulau Tekong, a small island off Singapore's northeast coast, to begin a weeks-long course of basic military training (BMT). Restricted usage of phones, limited contact with the outside world. Somewhere in this period is his 'wedding ceremony'. Each recruit is matched with a rifle. This is your 'wife'. She belongs to you now. And you belong to your country.

Singapore is one of the sixty-six countries in the world in which military training is mandatory. It was first introduced in 1967 when the British decided to withdraw all their troops from their Singapore bases, and the government found itself with a newly-independent country to protect. 'The most important thing is our defence,' said Lee Kuan Yew. For him, it was a simple question of 'survival or being destroyed by others'.[24]

Fight or flight. Provide and protect. Kill or be killed. Step up and be a man.

I find this a strange thing to contemplate when walking past the War Memorial Park, a tall, stone obelisk dedicated to the civilian victims of World War II. It's a weird thing to think that the neat-T-shirt-wearing, slick-haired office workers on their way to grab a sandwich from the nearby Raffles City mall or the floppy-haired teenagers in logo T-shirts skateboarding across the marble floors of the Esplanade underpass all learn how to annihilate enemies with their rifle wives.

'It's a rite of passage,' says Venky firmly. 'It's something every boy has to go through to become a Singaporean man.'

Venky—like any good Singaporean boy—left his family for the first time at eighteen to start BMT, serve his country, and marry his rifle. His everyday routine consisted of morning exercises, physical training (including a well-trodden obstacle course), weapons handling and firing, and field camp in the jungle. Occasionally, there was theory, with its eagerly welcomed air-conditioned classrooms.

Everyone is assigned to SCDF (Singapore Civil Defence Force), SPF (Singapore Police Force), or SAF (Singapore Armed Forces) before enlistment. After BMT, SAF recruits get assigned to vocations within the military, such as signaller, medic, or combat engineer.

The top BMT performers are selected to attend command schools (Officer Cadet School) or Specialist Cadet School where they receive training to become commissioner officers or sergeants, respectively, Venky explains.

Venky got transferred to the Air Force, where he worked as a signaller, operating the radio sets needed to relay communications on potentially 'hostile' aircrafts in Singapore airspace. It sounds like a *Top Gun* subplot, but he remembers 'being like a glorified clerk . . . with lots of mistakes. We forgot our radio telephony discipline and protocol all the time.'

He missed his freedom, his family. There was frustration at the curfew, at being separated from his bed. He missed functional plumbing.

'My most memorable moment of BMT was spending a week outfield in the jungle and doing my business in a latrine we'd dug with our shovels,' he remembers. 'By the end of the week, it was filled with so much human waste that it was impossible to go near.'

There were minor rebellions, fuelled by claustrophobia and routine. Rumours of recruits getting extras (army lingo for extra duties) for breaking curfew. Recruits getting extras for sneaking girls back into the barracks. Recruits getting extras for scrawling zany graffiti all over the dormitory walls in marker. Maybe it is a postcolonial thing, but Singapore military service never sounded so much like a British boarding school.

Upon completion of their statutory National Service obligations, NS graduates are tied to the forces on a reservist basis and are available to be enlisted for up to forty days of service yearly until the age of forty or fifty, depending on rank. You can also choose to enlist full-time as a serviceman, which I've heard anecdotally involves 'a lot of paperwork'.

Women are allowed to enlist in the military but are not subject to National Service. The economic cost of delaying the other half of the population from entering employment for two years would, according to Minister for Defence Ng Eng Hen, when addressing the issue in a 2022 parliamentary questions, come at a societal cost that would far outweigh the benefits.[25] Women have a different role in protecting the nation; one that involves upholding the workforce and family units.

Men around the world are fighting another, different battle, one where suicide is still a leading killer of men aged below forty-five. Of the deaths by suicide in 2023, almost 69 per cent, were male.[26]

Sabrina Ooi, founder of the mental health organization Calm Collective Asia, does not directly link NS and suicide but partly blames the two years of military training for perpetuating toxic masculine ideals.

'[Gender stereotypes] have been so deeply ingrained . . . the idea of the man having to be the breadwinner, having to save face and generally having to man up, it's still very much part of the psyche of Singaporeans in general,' she says. 'And I do wonder if it's because of things like having to go through NS, where you have to be a man.'

But Venky disagrees. The best thing he gained from his two years of military service wasn't a feeling of proud patriotism but a deeper sense of belonging through the friendships and camaraderie he established. We are worried about hurtling into a loneliness epidemic—surveys claim around one in five men have no close friends at all. NS is a time where you can form the sort of close bonds possible only through a once-in-a-lifetime experience, no matter how many open-pit bog holes that experience might contain.

No one in my family joined the forces, but growing up, I always felt a connection to the stories of 'army brats', the kids of military families transposing their lives through a series of identical barracks in different countries. I identified with their stories of new classrooms, new faces, unfamiliar accents, even though my dad's turf was the corporate trenches of risk derivatives.

'Military man?' people would sometimes ask when I told them we moved around a lot, and I would find it ironic that leaving your home country carried this assumption of patriotic loyalty.

I visit a family carnival hosted by the Singapore Armed Forces Reservists Association (SAFRA) to celebrate the recent opening of a new centre in Choa Chu Kang. The new building is all high modern walls, multi-tiered oblong blocks, and concrete plant-boxes dripping with vines. The crowded void deck is packed with trestle table stalls selling plastic trinkets and cutesy hair accessories that flash on the wearer's head like a roving satellite.

Children armed with darts launch stealth attacks on balloons pinned to targets while a teenager in a black volunteer T-shirt slowly spins cotton candy. As someone tries to coax me into a prize draw for a holographic night light, another volunteer ushers me out of the path of an oncoming dinky train. The air smells of fast food and is reverberating with Taylor Swift pounding from large speakers. She only stops for special guest Danny Koh, legendary local fire eater, to take to a small stage and gulp flames like hot popcorn, which is on sale from a nearby booth.

There are eight locations for SAFRA clubs including this newly launched one. For a fee of around $43, for three years, anyone who has served in the forces is eligible to access any of the clubs and their facilities. Choa Chu Kang is the first with a covered pool, an indoor climbing wall, and a 150-metre skyrunning track. They can sign up for continuing education courses and receive pro bono legal advice. They can sign their family members up for any of these perks too.

The atmosphere at Choa Chu Kang is more like a community carnival than a military gathering. These aren't people who want to die for their country. These are people who want to live for their country. Who want to relish in what makes it worth protecting. Food. Family. Love. No recently married rifles here.

We like to play soldiers. We like to use the language of war to show our love. I would do anything for you. I would fight for you. I would die. Though that is the point: it is only play. Singapore is one of the safest countries in the world. Its last war was over eighty years ago, though its spectres still linger in the neat units of Gillman Barracks or Dempsey, the former British stronghold named after a colonial commander-in-chief, updated as private galleries and trendy eateries.

Young Singaporean men leap obstacle courses and marry guns while, in other countries, hospitals are razed to the ground and pale-faced teenagers prepare to kill. Nothing trains you for war. Not really.

Macavity the Cat

There were rules to being young in a young country. Ideas of what was right, what was proper, what was wrong. Restrictions seeping through the pores of everyday life in the city. Singapore in the sixties and early seventies was a country of unbridled possibility built on a list of nos.

No long hairstyles on men
No *Playboy* magazine
No gongs and cymbals at Chinese wakes and funerals
No films, books, or comics depicting violence, sex, or gangsterism
No striptease performances
No jukebox lounges
No pirate taxis
No 'tikam takam' games of chance
No firecrackers
No smoking in the Cabinet Office, cinemas, or on buses
No advertising of cigarettes
No rock and roll music
No stepping out of line. No disobedience. No exceptions.[27]

No western long-haired hippies with their psychedelic drug culture, liberal sexual norms, and anti-establishment protests. No clandestine world of the Chinese gangs and secret societies with their loud musical traditions and vicious inter-group rivalries.

It was a national identity sharpened as an antithesis to outside and inside threats. Launched in the late fifties, an Anti-Yellow Cultural Council, led by the government and based on a phrase imported by schoolteachers from China to describe nepotism, gambling, and opium-smoking spreading pleasure and vice throughout their home country. I had always pegged 'yellow' as an insult used solely by white people. I had never realized it could also be used by yellow people turning in on themselves.

This Yellow Culture crackdown was not about colour, really. It clamped down on Hong Kong magazines and American comic books. It lasted decades. In the seventies, British rock band Led Zeppelin refused to cut their hair for a gig and were promptly sent back to England.

My mum grew up in this cautionary tale of don'ts and fears. She started roller-skating, cruising brake-free down the city's newly-laid, smooth streets. One day, she fell through a broken monsoon drain grill, peeling the skin from her ankle to shin like a wood shaving. The sutures hurt like hell, but the scar was brilliant.

She learned she was smart. This was a surprise. In primary school, her reports had been filled with red inked comments. *Not attentive enough. Must try harder.* Once, a teacher caught her frantically trying to erase mistakes with a spit-soaked finger and promptly hurled her exercise book out the window.

But her father had wanted smart children—the next generation's success in a country he had squeezed himself into like a wrong puzzle piece, dreaming a future for his children from the negative space of opportunities he never had.

She managed to be top of her class in the Singapore Cambridge examinations and won a place at Raffles Institution. The white stone building was an establishment of Singaporean success. The students' parents were part of the right private members' clubs. They had the right jobs in government or in the top rafters of industry. Singapore was a country built determinedly on meritocracy. Working hard could get you far. Working hard in the right institutions could get you even further.

'There were other girls from other schools who got in,' my mum remembers. 'A group of musically talented women gladiators from Marymount Convent, a girls' Catholic school. They boasted a future well-known Singapore singer and a government minister's daughter.'

She had her own gang—her best friend Jacqueline; Barbara, a small and round pocket rocket; and a girl they only knew as 'Smelly Peggy'. They were a motley crew bonding over a shared love of twenties music, and when the annual Raffles Institution Drama festival was announced, they wrote a short teenage musical of a thwarted love story, complete with costumes handmade using satin and sequins from Arab Lane.

'We thought we did a pretty good job,' says mum. The Marymount girls chose a dance rendition of T.S. Eliot's poem 'Macavity: The Mystery Cat', performed in all black leotards. 'They would arrange themselves in a pyramidal group, voicing different segments of the poem individually in a dramatic and highly professional, choreographed set piece.'

The stage was set for battle, but the night before the performance, the principal received a notice. The festival was open to the general public, and the government had certain protocols on what was age and audience appropriate. No shoulder straps. No bare shoulders. No twenties' high kicks. 'We got a formal notice that our little play did not fit the rigorous standards of Singapore sensitivities. We were banned for actions unbecoming at the age of fifteen.'

Another crackdown. Another refusal. Another no. This time at a personal micro-level. She left Singapore soon after that.

I've heard this story before. It crops up at the occasional family dinner. My mum brings it up once every few years, like a forgotten family tradition or an unexpected guest at a party. Even she seems slightly surprised she still remembers it. But it's the cumulation of small memories that shape us. If we're all the stars of our own stage show, then everything is a potential plot twist, part of a character arc, building blocks onto an unfinished being.

I like the way the story ends too. The pushback. The argument with the principal that involved both my mum and my grandfather. A father stepping in for what his daughter believed in, even if he didn't really understand it. The last minute repeal.

'We got the go-ahead!,' my mum remembers. 'We performed and I had a blast. The audience loved it.'

'But, of course, Macavity the bloody cat got the prize.'

A COUNTRY'S TAPESTRY

I ♥ Hawkers

Food is a big deal in Singapore. How much of a big deal? Instead of saying 'How are you?' it is common to hear friends and colleagues ask each other, 'Have you eaten?' Heated debates over where you can get the perfect fiery-sweet sambal sauce dominate small talk and cyberspace. 'Café hopping', the gastronomical cousin of Britain's pub hopping, is a legitimate hobby: forging a trail through a local area's restaurants one course at a time, before staggering home at closing time, dreading tomorrow's food hangover. That's how big a deal it is.

'We think and feel with our stomachs,' a Singaporean friend once told me. Over lunch.

When Paul and I first arrive in Singapore, we are warned about the 'Singapore Stone', an ominous albatross of extra weight that hangs uncomfortably visible, the sign of too good a time, or too many tangy pineapple tarts. I avoid weighing scales like the climax of a horror movie or a looming deadline and tuck in.

There are over 5,000 restaurants on the island, specializing in almost every cuisine from around the world. You can feast on flaky shreds of duck wrapped in a pastilla parcel of buttery crisp filo pastry in Tanjong Pagar. You can crunch cubes of spicy seasoned watermelon in Lavender. You can nibble on Peranakan cake dyed cocoa-brown from *buah keluak*, a rich dark nut laced with cyanide. Crabs claw their way up the sides of crowded tanks along Boat Quay as touts shout happy hour deals in your face.

And this is before you even hit the hawkers.

Hawker centres are the king of Singapore's culinary kingdom. These open-air food complexes are caverns of clanging woks, hissing oil, and the smell of a jazz symphony of spices as competing stalls clash and jive together.

Many have a 'family recipe'. Many are a jealously-guarded secret. There is always one generic western food stall that can be relied on to have chips.

Singapore's hawker centres are known well outside the Lion City. UNESCO crowned hawker culture the country's first element on their list of Intangible Cultural Heritage of Humanity in December 2020. International food stars have visited and lavished them with praise. Gordon Ramsay's scowling face is stuck to his favourite chicken rice stall in Maxwell's Food Centre, like a grumpy winner's rosette. Anthony Bourdain, the late rockstar of food and travel writing, deemed them ' . . . wonderlands of Chinese, Indian, and Malay specialties.'

But no matter how well you think you know them from international renown, there is nothing that can replicate from afar the flaming heat from the rusty open-air grills on Satay Street, fed by the owner's wide wicker fan. There is nothing to emulate the smooth feel of the crayon-bright plastic table under your fingers, slightly sticky from the memories of past meals, or the first surprising bite of black carrot cake—no carrots, but crunchy, chewy, wok-fried Chinese radish, seasoned with soy sauce and tossed with ribbons of sunny yellow egg. You have to be there.

We gorge our way through these Aladdin's caves of new flavours. The double tiers of Amoy Street, where colleagues sit on long communal tables and pick black pepper beef from fluffy pillows of steamed rice. Spicy 'red oil' dumplings under the arched gable of Maxwells. Chomp Chomp, where Paul picks a fresh fish from a stony-eyed shoal of seafood lying on a bed of ice, and it appears fifteen minutes later, lightly grilled, tasting like the ocean, with a bright orange dollop of sambal chilli paste glowing like a tiny angry sun. Geylang Serai market, one of the few centres with a high proportion of halal food stalls, where creamy hard-boiled quails' eggs are marinated in belacan chilli, lemon juice, ginger, garlic, and a dash of tomato sauce. Lau Pa Sat, where colonial wives used to shop for their seafood. Other well-loved hawker markets can be found in Newton and on Old Airport Road.

Once, each of these hawkers would have been one-man bands, carrying their ingredients and wares, ready to whip up a dish on-site and on-demand. Now, they are all part of a greater whole, a buzzing centre with its own atmosphere and personality.

Paul is a natural at hawker centres. He tries everything and loves it all, apart from the creamy pungent flesh of durian, a fruit so smelly it's banned on public transport. Hawker aunties love him. They come and coo over him, complimenting his dinner choices, happy at the simple sight of someone gobbling with such gusto.

'You!' one tiny grey-haired diner said, pointing at my husband as he happily hoovered up a brown hillock of duck braised rice, 'Look like Prince George.' She then turned to me and mimed a swelling movement over her stomach, which could have indicated getting full or that I'd better nail this one down quick and have babies.

There is a delicate network of etiquette around hawker centres. You don't have to clean your table, but you should always return your tray. Leave a small item on an empty table, a business card or a pack of tissues, and the table is 'chop'd' (reserved), and you win the right to cold stare at anyone who takes that seat. The elderly seem to be exempt from chope rules: respect for older generations trumps food centre manners, and Auntie trumps your chair.

The accessibility of affordable food at hawker centres has led to a rumour among expats that Singaporeans don't cook. This is fuelled by the small kitchenettes, with virgin-clean two-ring hobs and sad plug-in ovens in some of the business district condominiums. Imported produce—which is about 90 per cent of the country's foodstuffs—is pricey on the supermarket shelves.

It is also a rumour that has caused huge offence to any Singaporean I've been foolish enough to float it by, and rightly so. Of course people who love food this much can cook. And at the right wet markets, at the right time, i.e. early in the morning, and with the right haggling skills, you can get a price that beats the commercial conglomerates.

I've wondered if there's an aftertaste of progressive discrimination that fuels these false tales of culinary incompetence: the famous chef and Singapore's food ambassador Violet Oon claimed that the women's liberation movement where 'women . . . were not only burning the bra, they threw away the wok', is the reason she's one of the few women of her generation who cooks professionally.[28]

But the truth is, when there's the pull of dozens of different flavours at your doorstep, with the added attraction of no washing up, it's tempting to hunt down a hawker meal. Out of the kitchen and into the wild.

We explore outside the hawker centres too. We eat lightly grilled white toast seeping with slabs of butter and sweet *kaya* coconut jam at kopitiams, small alfresco coffee shops. I attend a Teochew baking class in Sembawang, where after munching on brittle sweet peanut candy and flaky red-bean *da lao bing*, 'son-in-law' biscuits, all part of the *xi bing* wedding confectionery, I manage to overbake a rainbow mooncake to its crispy death.

But the allure of the hawkers is persistent, like the smell of fresh cooking to a hungry stomach. I love their noise. I love the thick loaded plates holding a hodgepodge of fried egg slices, squares of silky tofu, and round coins of sweet Chinese sausage on a bed of vermicelli noodles, or sweet meat rolls of *ngoh hiang*, Hokkien comfort food at its finest and the ultimate hangover cure. I love the soft, flaky flesh of barbequed stingray and the surprising crunch of *kueh pie tee,* crispy pastry shells housing a filling of finely sliced vegetables.

I love the people watching too. The crisp-shirted businessman asleep on crossed forearms in front of a bowl of tawny laksa broth, rich with coconut milk, fish balls bobbing like buoys tangled in thin rice noodles. The boisterous families fighting over grilled skewers by the open flames of Satay Street.

Maybe it's the overall sense of inclusivity, that there's space at these plastic tables for everyone. Bourdain said it in his book *Medium Raw*, when he posits, 'The hawker centre could be the answered prayer for every hard-pressed office worker in a hurry, every blue-collar worker on a budget, every cop on a lunch hour, as well as obsessive foodies at every income level.' Tommy Koh, diplomat and lawyer who was Singapore's permanent representative to the United Nations at various points from the sixties to the eighties, said it too.

'The open air hawker centres and the air-conditioned food courts of Singapore are places where all social classes and income groups eat together. Food is a great social leveller in Singapore,' he writes in the book, *There's No Carrot in Carrot Cake*, a showcase of Singaporean street food.

It's not perfect. The options catering to specific religious requirements are arguably not as widespread or accessible as they should be in a proudly multi-faith society. But there's something greater than the sum of ingredients in a hawker centre, something that goes deeper than a good meal. Some call it 'Asian style', this chaotic communal way of eating you see in almost all hawker centres; the happy groups sharing a medley of different dishes with roots in different ethnic cuisines, but still different from anything in their country of origin, entirely and deliciously Singaporean. Others call it 'family style'.

A Beng Who Cooks

This is not a restaurant review. If it were, I'd comment on the concrete walls of the small, moodily-lit shophouse off Duxton, shadowy except for the spotlight on the restaurant's name. It's stuck to the wall in bulging bold black letters under their logo of a shark-like sleek kitchen knife.

The letters say, 'Beng Who Cooks', a nod to the Singlish slang '*beng*' for working-class flashy geezers, Singapore's 'chavs', a shout-out to those who are outsiders in the city's high-achieving society and social ideals. If this were a restaurant review I'd mention the tableware, ceramic glazed inky tones of urban hip. It would also be a good idea to talk about the food. But because this isn't a restaurant review, the first and main thing I notice is Jason, one of the main bengs behind the enterprise, who envelops me in a tight tattooed hug, despite the fact that we're total strangers. I've read about him, though. The articles about the outspoken teenager whose tattoos got him kicked out of home by his parents. 'For a kid at fifteen, being thrown out, it causes a mark,' he remarked candidly as we sat over dark ceramic bowls of snowy swimmer crab. 'We didn't really repair it for a long time.'

Food is in Jason's blood and hawkering is in his roots. His parents owned a fruit stall and, with the long hours spent feeding customers, often had little time to feed the family. Cooking didn't start as a passion, it was a way to survive.

He honed his skills through his teenage years living with his grandmother, and at twenty-four, became Singapore's youngest hawker, serving poke bowls in Chinatown's Hong Lim Complex. There, among crowds of people his parents' age, he found a sort of substitute family and a community.

'Food is something [that makes] people gather together, eat together, talk through a dinner or lunch,' he says. 'The spirit of a hawker is actually a spirit that binds together. Especially because everybody's stall is so small.'

Nostalgia is a common seasoning throughout the restaurant, which he opened in 2020 with his partner, former MMA fighter, Hung Zhen Long. Each dish has a memory and a meaning. The moreish sea-salt fried broccoli was created in a bid to get his high-school sweetheart to enjoy vegetables. They're now married and recently had a son who they nicknamed 'Cabbage'. Jason has the Chinese characters for the vegetable tattooed across his neck.

Unlike most western cultures, food in Asia is dripping with the sauce of symbolism. Long noodles for long life. Dumplings shaped like gold or silver ingots.

It's also a cliché that Asian parents say, 'I love you,' not through words but with full mouths and heaped plates, a silent promise that 'You'll never go hungry. Not if I have anything to do with it.' My mum is like this. Even now, my friends refer to her as a 'feeder'. Every serving of carefully-shredded beef dripping with thick oyster sauce, every scalding tray of sweet soy-baked chicken was her saying 'I care', with forced second and third helpings. Lil Sis and I seem to have inherited this. It's like a generational tic.

Jason's father was a typical 'old-school Asian father', hard-working, reticent, and sparse with outward affection. It wasn't until later, when he'd slowly reestablished bonds with his parents, that he found out that his father had lost the fruit stall during the 2008 financial crisis and had silently juggled a number of ad-hoc jobs to put food on the table.

I asked Jason what his favourite dish on the Beng Who Cooks' menu was. He pointed to an unusual addition, a vibrant medley of orange and passionfruit with cubes of fresh salmon ceviche resting on top of a papadum.

'I'm very familiar with fruits,' he said simply. 'And now I realize my parents worked so hard for petty cash to feed myself and my brother. So, it's my way of saying, "Thank you."'

Percy

I have swallowed a brick. I can feel it settling somewhere between my breastbone and large intestine. Making its way to settle in the cement of my already full stomach. I have overdone it. This was a mistake. And it was worth every bite.

Sugee cake is a heady blend of almonds, semolina, eggs, and brandy, whipped together and baked for special occasions, such as Christmas or the end of a really good meal. It can be topped with toasted almonds or marzipan, adding a layer of sweetness to the richness. It is heavy as a lump of sand, comfortingly moreish, and a staple dessert of Eurasian cuisine. This is what Percy assures me when he insists on ordering a slice.

Percy is gentle-mannered, with betel nut black eyes and a thick ice-white beard that makes him look a bit like Santa. He has played Santa at community festivals. He's played a lot of roles in his seventy-five years: a senior admin security officer, a chef, a volunteer working with prison inmates and vulnerable communities. Currently, he is chairman of the Eurasian Heritage Society and an avid detective of his own Eurasian lineage.

There are around 18,000 Eurasians in Singapore, less than 1 per cent of the total population. They are a small and complex blend of the East and West. The first wave of Portuguese settlers arrived in the region in the sixteenth century, spreading their Christian religion and dance moves. The British introduced cricket and shepherd's pie to the region and brought many Eurasians into the ranks of white-collar civil service. The seventeenth century Dutch settled mostly around the Malacca and Ceylon regions around the same period. Each wave weaving threads of tradition, faith, and food into this hybrid tapestry of culture.

Percy's paternal ancestors were British free mariners who arrived at the Straits of Malacca in the eighteenth century and settled there, which generally means finding a nice local lady to start a family with. His mother's forefathers were from a prominent Portuguese clan that had roots in the Straits settlements dating back to the 1500s.

'Eurasians were very quiet about their identity. Growing up, our parents did not talk to us about our history,' he says. For snippets of heritage, he relied on the church, the Catholic religion the Portuguese settlers brought with them, or muffled conversations in Kristang, a creole of Portuguese and the local Malaccan dialect, which he would listen to through closed doors after bedtime.

'It was like a secret code,' Percy remembers. 'But we learned all the swear words!'

But food was never a secret. Food is one of the first things Percy remembers. His mother ran a food stall on the banks of Boat Quay, and there he learned the skills of the trade from his school days. He would accompany her to the market and learn how to select the best ingredients. Back home, he would practise the repetitive and satisfying grind of pounding chillies.

'So many chillies. People don't realize Eurasian food has so much,' Percy warns me.

Maybe it was baked into his fate that Percy would start his career as a cook. One day, while he was working as a mess clerk at the British officers' mess in Tanglin, a captain approached Percy and asked about his last name. Shepherdson didn't sound very . . . Asian to this chipper Brit. But, he reassured Percy, 'There are lots of Shepherdsons in England.'

Eurasian food, like Eurasian culture itself, is a hybrid of cultures, a melting pot of ingredients and techniques. Beef *smore* is a thick meaty stew, cooked with soy sauce and served with steamed rice or crumbled scones. Devil curry, not of Satanic origins, but from the Kristang word for leftovers—'*debal*'—simmers Christmas scraps with candlenut, mustard seed, and galangal, ginger's citrusy sister. Noodles, spicy and stir-fried, are served with pineapple chutney and topped with squid and shrimp.

They used to call the Portuguese 'shrimp people', Percy says, due to the fact they caught more of the pink crustaceans than anyone else along the Malacca Straits.

We share some of these dishes as Percy shares his history in the Eurasian Association's restaurant, Quentin's, named after Quentin Pereira, one of the Lion City's few Eurasian chefs. The multi-course meal is inspired by Pereira's grandparents' recipes. We try pork *semur*, simmering in a broth of carrots, onions, and ginger with fried rice speckled with salty corned beef next to a glossy fried egg.

As we chew on inky black calamari, Percy tells me how he fell in love.

She was a Chinese Buddhist from a traditional conservative family. He was a Eurasian Catholic born on Good Friday. Her parents disapproved.

It wasn't the religion Percy believes. For them, Eurasians reminded them of the memories of Europeans, their love for dancing and partying, against the grain of their traditional hardworking ideals.

They married in 1977. Percy's new in-laws didn't attend the wedding, but his wife's siblings did.

He never forgot the British captain's words. They nagged, reminding him of how little he knew about his heritage. Shortly after his wedding, he embarked on a mission try to track down all the Shepherdsons they could find in the region and England. Shepherdsons came out of the woodwork from America. From Australia.

Percy was not related to any of them.

'We were on our own in Singapore. The last Shepherdsons,' he said.

The final strands of his bloodline in Britain had died in Durham in the 1700s. For three centuries, they had stayed in the north of England, except for one Captain Matthew Shepherdson, who sailed for further adventures to the East in 1792. Percy went on a trip to Durham with his nephew Kevin to search for the land of his ancestors. In the crisp Yorkshire air, he felt a sense of home.

'You can feel the coldness of winter,' he recalls. 'You can feel the shadow of your forefathers. It was beautiful.'

Food and identity are a constant juggling act for Singapore Eurasians, like the Jinkli Nona dance, a blend of Singaporean, Portuguese, Malaccan, and Macanese influences with joyful accordion accompaniment. It's fighting for acceptance from other cultures while managing to maintain your own ethnic identity in a country where you make up less than a hundredth of its people.

Percy's book, *Journey to the Straits: The Shepherdson Story* has become one of the main Singaporean works on Eurasian history. He's one of the first Eurasians to produce a book on Eurasian genealogy. Our meal in the Eurasian centre is constantly interrupted by people who greet him like close relatives.

Both his daughters have married into local Chinese Singaporean families and, unlike his in-laws, Percy feels this is exactly the way it should be—preserving your heritage's culture and traditions, while your bloodline naturally dilutes into the plasma of a wider national identity. The last of the itinerant Shepherdsons, the first of a new family line, assimilated outsiders, carving their own small niche in this small country.

At the launch of the book, around 200 family members gathered, a crowd of local Lion City Shepherdsons, coming together to celebrate, commemorate, and of course, eat.

'At the end of the day, I am Singaporean first and Eurasian second,' he tells me, fork loaded with a mound of Sugee cake. 'You can be both.'

Bad British Asian

One thing we don't gorge ourselves on is dim sum. Not that we don't like dim sum. There's just a ubiquitousness about it that has sucked it of its novelty, like a plain pork ball without its shiny dumpling casing. I like dim sum just fine. To admit otherwise would be to condemn myself to the nadir of being a 'Bad British Asian'.

I learn this from *I'm a Bad Asian*, a YouTube comedy mini-series created by film producer Philip Wang's Wong Fu productions. In it, Andrew, the Asian American main character, commits the ultimate cultural sacrilege: he doesn't like dim sum.

'That's like a black guy that doesn't like soul food or a white girl that doesn't like cold-pressed juice,' say his horrified friends. 'It's ingrained in your culture. You have to at least pretend.'

Do all Asian diaspora kids feel this? Like with every move, every preference, every bite, we are falling short of the expectations of our heritage? Maybe it's because, in the West, we East and Southeast Asians in particular have been generalized as the 'well-behaved', 'quiet' ethnic minority that the trope of being a 'bad 'Asian is alive and kicking its own cliché around the internet.

I turn to the closest Bad British Asian I know: Lil Sis. They say there's nothing like the closeness of a sibling bond to share in everything, even a collective sense of cultural guilt.

Here is the list we come up with (specific to our British East Asian heritage). It takes us less than ten minutes:

1. Not being able to speak Mandarin
2. Not working in one of the magical 'big four': finance, engineering, medicine, law

3. Not having any extended family nearby (how do we honour our Confucian values?)
4. Never bringing home a nice Chinese boy from a good family
5. Not being good at maths
6. Not enjoying bubble tea
7. The fact that our home-made dumplings look like Shrek in a car crash

We're laughing at this point, partly from disastrous memories of sporadic family dumpling-making gatherings—doughy flour skins pressed into grotesque blobs, pink mincemeat flying like a circus abattoir—but also because we are falling back on lazy dated stereotypes and we know it. We are taking the caricatures society has heaped on us and turning them against ourselves.

This should feel more subversive than it does. Instead, it just feels silly.

We are very different, Lil Sis and me. She is organized to my scatty, cynical to my obtusely trusting, cool to my retriever puppy exuberant. She has the oval face, the soft prettiness of my mum's side of the family. More Chow than Oon. I am a mongrel mutt: high cheekbones, square jaw, big butt, duck feet. I don't really resemble anyone in my family, but if I had to stake my claim, I suppose I look a bit like Dad. Still, since Mum dressed us in matching pinafores, we have been a double force, even when I pushed her off our bunk bed or she smashed her new Lego set over my skull. I love her with a fierce intensity, despite her enviable guitar skills. I love her despite the fact she's been taller than me since she was twelve.

Lil Sis went to a boarding school in the Oxfordshire countryside at seven while I stayed home in London. Her friends had ruddy cheeks and chipper accents and spent weekends riding horses in Bampton. She was athletic, outdoorsy, and self-deprecating with a dash of the stiff upper lip. At eighteen, she won a place to study Classics at Cambridge.

'I guess I was trying consciously to not fall into those Asian stereotypes,' she remembers. 'I mean, I studied Classics, which is quite possibly the whitest British thing you can do. I think I really wanted to fit in in the places I felt most intrinsically different, the most "British institutions".'

We've both done this, overcompensating for the differences our skin might give away. It's an old diaspora trick. Most of us have tried to fold ourselves into the cultures that have taken us in, scrubbing out our differences that our parents or grandparents have carried across the border. Lil Sis and I are lucky, two pampered middle-class kids from nice schools. Those whiter than white echelons of Britishness never seemed inaccessible to us, even if they hinted that we might never really belong.

'I live halfway across the world from all of my relatives,' says Lil Sis. '[And] if I'm distant from that, and distant from my roots, it's become a piece of me that I kind of have to just put in the back of my mind.'

We've gone the opposite direction too. Fed up with the nunchucks jokes, the catcalls of '*Ni hao*', and '*Konnichiwa*', the work emails addressed to the only other Asian employee in the company, we've stuck a middle finger up to assimilation and thrown ourselves into evening Mandarin classes and signed up for school team hoodies emblazoned with our Chinese middle names.

But without an anchor to our heritage, we were just floating around in a sea of distant cultural references. Is that partly what I hoped to find in Singapore? Some flotsam of identity I relate to, to make me feel less British, more Asian, less bad?

If so, I am sorely disappointed. I am cheerfully referred to as 'so banana' by Asian friends at dinner parties, yellow on the outside, white on the inside. It took moving to Asia to realize how painfully, inerasably British I am.

I visit the site of my grandmother's house on MacPherson Road, a neat row of neat two-storey houses, tiled roofs sloping at identical angles. They're as familiar as strangers. If anything, the fact that my mother grew up here and left, sometimes makes me seem more alien, a family who had roots here but willingly gave them up. And now, like an annoying seasonal jingle or a *Terminator*-era Arnold Schwarzenegger, I am back.

The more I settle into this country that housed my grandparents and parents the more I realize that I am even further from my heritage—an even 'worse' Asian—than I thought.

'Race is a social construct,' says Aaron K. H. Ho, lecturer and Minority Studies specialist at Nanyang Technological University in his book, *"Is It Because I'm Chinese?": Chinese Privilege in Singapore.*[29] 'Notions about race are created by humans in society . . . we are telling stories about ourselves and as stories pass down from generations to generations, stories become inaccurate, false and full of gaps.'

Ho reminds us, 'Louisiana counted Chinese as white for census prior to 1870, and, after that, Chinese became blacks not Asians.' What it means to 'be Chinese' or 'be Asian' has shifted across different countries and periods. The benchmarks of ethnicity are defined by the country's majority, or the stories and expectations fed to us by our families.

And the bar keeps shifting. In *I'm A Bad Asian*, Andrew's younger cousin complains, 'Now, thanks to all these dance crew shows and K-Pop and YouTube, everyone thinks Asians can dance. *In addition* to being smart.'

I definitely can't dance. I am not that smart. But I do know that nagging feeling of constantly falling short. The squeezing insecurity of never being quite good enough. I don't think this is unique to immigrant and diaspora families, though perhaps it's more common among these communities. The pressure of what previous generations gave up. The tenuous links to a country we don't know.

At school, spooked that the apex of being smart, polished, well-behaved was something I could never reach, I kicked back. I played up, spoke out of turn, tore expectations down before I had a chance to miss them. But deep inside, I too wanted to play it safe. I clowned around to win approval. I crammed anxiously and secretly to get good grades. I was cocky and sometimes rude, but I cried when I felt I'd let my parents or teachers down. A part of me still wanted to be a 'Good' Asian.

Thank God for sisters. Thank God for someone to share the load with. To make you feel less alone. And to laugh over a dumpling that's strange-looking and clumsily made but tastes hot and comforting and exactly as it should.

Singlish Rules

I have a secret weapon, a little bottle of shock factor I whip out for special occasions or whenever I open my mouth. Lil Sis has it too; we share it with a number of other Asian diaspora Brits freckled across the country.

We look Asian but we sound English. What's more, we sound 'posh English', the sort that's moulded from scholarship access to the hushed gothic quads of British public schools, where lacrosse is character building, and we learn to separate our Aeschylus from our Aristophanes.

'You speak so well for an Asian!' people say to us, which, ironically, is one of the only times words fail me.

Sometimes, this works against us, a generation of slick-tongued Etonians in government hasn't done wonders for toffs' credibility. Most of the time, though, it's helped more than it's hindered me. People have assumed I'm smarter, richer, more sober than I actually am, based on an accent I've done nothing to earn. My current account might look more like the average age of a premier league footballer than their bank balance, but I speak—as my colleague Anas once pointed out—like I have a silver spoon stuck up my arse.

In Singapore, like in many countries, the way you speak can give a clue about your background. There are the light RP inflections of expensive private schools with colonial names like Raffles Institution or Anglo-Chinese School. There are the Australian or American twangs of the internationally educated. But there is one common bond, a crazy, sharp, clever code that transcends class and calibre, the badge of identity of a true blue Singaporean, and that is Singlish.

Singlish is not one of the four official languages of Singapore, but it arguably speaks louder than English, Tamil, Malay, or Mandarin ever will. A melting pot of a dialect for a melting pot of a nation, it stirs flavours of Hokkien, Teochew, Cantonese, Malay, and Tamil into a punchy English stock. It's the perfect creole for idle banter with friends, or, as the Singlish connoisseur would say, 'talking cock'.

'It's a very efficient language,' says Venky sagely. 'It allows for focus on more important things in life, like what to eat and getting smashed. Speaking of getting smashed, that's "*mabuk*", in Singlish. It's a Malay word.'

Such a *rojak* language can be easy to *sotong*. But even if you don't *play play,* speaking Singlish can make you seem more *ah beng* than *atas*. Singlish is the word on the street, a world of smashed vowels and elisions away from the express streams of elite schoolrooms. True Singlish natives know how to code switch, steering their way from Singlish to English, seamlessly swimming in any social pool.

You wouldn't use Singlish in a job interview. But you might crack it out in a business meeting, at an elusive sweet spot, to ease the formality and cement rapport. Singlish can smooth the edges of a conversation or add its spikes.

'I think we wait until end of quarter to double confirm, lah,' says my gentle colleague at an internal meeting, effortlessly swaying the ranks and pouring water on any sizzling tensions. 'Save face, can or not?'

'$145?' shrieks a wispy-haired uncle, in a furious bargaining tussle with a fellow flip-flopped silver-haired senior, on a pair of narrow plastic stools inside Tiong Bahru market. 'Makes my stomach all fall out the back, lor.' This is accompanied by an alarmingly vivid hand miming violent diarrhoea.

The top echelons have a conflicted relationship with Singlish. The country's second prime minister Goh Chok Tong lambasted it as an 'English corrupted by Singaporeans . . . sprinkled with words and phrases . . . which English speakers outside Singapore have difficulties in understanding.' He launched the 'Speak Good English' movement in 2000, with programmes and activities focused on bumping out Singlish with the rounded vowels of British Standard English.

But from the seed of insecurity over being the pidgin English Asian on the global stage sprouts a perverse sense of pride. Singlish is a localized English, a common code that creates rapport and camaraderie with its fusion phrases. It's a way of taking the leftovers of British legacy and turning it into something new, different, our own. Even the government is mellowing, recognizing the co-existence of Singlish and 'proper' English and launching national tourism campaigns lauding the Lion City's *shiok* highlights and businesses inviting visitors to *lim kopi*.

'It's just a way of life for us,' a diner at the Amoy Street hawker market tells me over a steaming bowl of fish porridge. 'Our pace of life is so quick, Singlish means we can simplify and get our message across fast!'

When Luke Lu was a secondary school teacher in the early noughties, he used Singlish as a way to bond with his students. He was quickly reprimanded by his head of department. Now, as an assistant professor at Nanyang Technological University, he centres his research around the pedagogical value of Singlish.

For him, part of what has solidified Singlish's staying power is that, unlike in British English, there is no specific slang, no specific accent that sets apart a region or class. Despite a universal understanding that you wouldn't use it in certain professional settings, 'Singlish is actually used by everyone of all social classes.'

In fact, this has led to a certain inverse snobbishness against those who don't know how or refuse to use Singlish in the right settings. 'Especially among the youth, it's become a sort of lingua franca,' explains Lu. 'So if you only use the standard form of English, in [a] university group kind of setting, it's very likely that you won't have many friends.'

In Singapore, a country of different races, languages, and cultures, where almost everyone is bilingual and languages are taught and spoken within ethnic divides—Mandarin for the Chinese, Tamil for the Indians, Malay for the Malays—Singlish is common ground, a way of saying we're all together in this many-sided, fast-changing country, whether you're nation-born or a new arrival.

Ritu Jain moved to Singapore in 2000. She describes herself as a language 'purist', and when we speak on the phone, her voice is clear, crisp, with the accent-less tones of the true nomadic citizen of the world. An academic who specializes in language policy and planning, she was keen to teach communication through the strict grammatical rules of her international boarding school English. After imparting such wisdom at a Singaporean maritime association, she recalls that the mariners listened to her politely, then one told her, 'You can teach us all this, but it's not going to change a single thing. You think I'm going to ask a friend, "Would you like to go to lunch?" as opposed to "Eh, makan?"'

When she decided to make Singapore her permanent home, Jain the purist started to learn Singlish. She learned it from her children, who'd learned it from their friends on the playground. She learned it from the students she taught at Nanyang Technological University. It was part of her journey of becoming part of the family, a 'proper' Singaporean.

'If you want to belong, you must have some form of similarity, connection, alliance. You have to break the barriers somehow,' she explains. 'English is simply not our language, it's everyone's language. So we can't claim it. Only Singlish can be a unifier.'

Class Concepts

Orchard Road used to be a sprawling fertile ground of fruit orchards, pepper farms, and nutmeg plantations. Now it's sown the seeds of retail therapy and has sprouted a healthy crop of mega malls. There's Ion, a futuristic capsule of polygon panes, interlocking like scales. There's Ngee Ann City, a huge Orwellian structure in red marble, resembling Chinese tombstones. There's the curved temple gables of Tangs, the curved glass unicorn of Wheelock Place.

Most of these are interconnected by a maze of underground tunnels, veins pumping blood through the city's commercial heart. You can shop without ever seeing sunlight.

In Britain, as much as we'd like to deny it, class is woven deep into the thread of Britain's musty social tapestry. It's baked into our history, kneaded into medieval feudal systems, rising in the hot oven of Victorian industrialism and its burgeoning middle class.

But in Singapore, it should be different. Singapore is a young country, unencumbered by historical feudal systems. The first land rights divisions we had were the ones the British gave us, and Raffles allotted land according to ethnicity more than social standing.

From 2016–2017 a 3,000 person survey on Social Capital—the first of its kind on the Red Dot—was conducted, it reared an ugly surprise.[30] The study by the Institute of Policy Studies (IPS) revealed that social divides between Singaporeans could be influenced by class over race or religion.[31]

Maybe the apple doesn't fall as far from the colonial tree as I thought.

Class is a relatively recent concept for this young country. There are no centuries of feudal history that have accumulated generations of land and assets. 'Old money' is only decades old, unless it travelled with migrant families from their home countries. And, as anyone who's wandered behind the fishbowl glass walls of The Shoppes at Marina Bay Sands can observe, it mingles alongside 'new money', if not as friends, then at least as cordial acquaintances who would cheek kiss at a cocktail party. Inside these sloping towers, the bustle is hushed by the sounds of a whirlpool fountain and the current of a duck-egg blue artificial canal lapping against brightly coloured sampan boats as they ferry shoppers through corridors of tastefully branded designer boutiques.

You can flash your bling but only the right sort. *Ah bengs* are looked down on for their showy love of designer brands. In January 2023, seventeen-year-old Zoe Gabriel was trolled on social media for gushing over her 'luxury bag' birthday gift from her father, from high street brand Charles & Keith.

'I think it's mainly because Singapore's so young,' suggests my friend Stephanie. 'Especially the generations that made their wealth post-World War II wanted to show they could "make it" and buy nice things. This probably links to a lot of economic and infrastructure developments in the nineties: more professional jobs, the Asian Tiger economy, [and] more malls and buildings and roads being built.'

In this multicultural meritocracy, there is a deep-rooted narrative that whoever you are, everyone has a shot at the Singaporean dream of the five Cs: cash, car, credit card, condominium, and country club membership. But with that opportunity comes the price of pressure. If society sends the message that anyone can make it, you have no one to blame but yourself if you don't.

And even though Singaporeans might increasingly scoff at the concept of these five Cs as dated, they've bred a rat-race twitching with anxiety, a progressive competitiveness coupled with a traditional culture that has dedicated prayers, gods, and worship to the goals of wealth and prosperity or fate. The queues to any nondescript branch of Singapore Pools snakes around street corners every Sunday with eager hopefuls waiting to place their bets.

I've heard when a car crash happens in the city, passers-by slow down in case the licence plate is fate telling them the next week's lottery numbers.

And what about those who slip beneath the surface in a country where class seems inextricably linked to a sense of belonging, where 76 per cent of 'upper class' residents felt 'proud to be Singaporean' compared to 50 per cent of their 'lower class' peers?[32]

Homelessness 'doesn't exist' in Singapore, in that there's no official definition of it in the country's legislation, the closest you get is 'destitute person'. It's also an invisible phenomenon, the police have the right to take anyone found destitute on the streets into their charge.[33]

Still, Singapore's first study into its homeless residents in 2019 found between 921 and 1,050 rough sleepers living in the city-state.[34] The second, published in 2022, registered 616 in 2021, a 41 per cent drop, but the number of those living in a temporary shelter jumped from 65 to 420.[35]

Singapore is a country of immigrants after all, and as such, is built on the original immigrant mindset: work hard and earn so you can provide a better life for your children. Wealth trickling down like the old social structures of certain colonial forefathers.

I snake through the underground labyrinth of Orchard's malls early one Saturday morning on the way to a breakfast meeting.

Cross-legged on the tiled floors sit the weekend workers, tribes designated by their uniformed T-shirts, picking at Tupperware box breakfasts with plastic forks. It's a moment of calm before the retail tsunami. In a few minutes, Orchard Road will come alive. Businesses will open; deals will close. In a few minutes, this silence will be replaced with the pinball sounds of a thousand people searching for a better handbag, a better image, a better life.

The silence through the wide walkways, the dim corridor lights, and the shuttered shops gives the sense of a hallowed quiet. It's like a church before a service or the pause before a natural disaster.

Words Words Words

I am in the school library.

I can't remember which one, because it is a truth universally acknowledged that, at some level, most school libraries are the same—the same long plywood shelves, the same faint smell of disinfectant, sports kits, and crisps. That's a riff off Jane Austen, but I haven't discovered Austen yet. I am twelve years old, or maybe ten. My friends are Amy March, Roald Dahl's magical genius Matilda, and an angry, brave teenager called Alys who lives in a fictional Ukrainian city racked by Chernobyl.

I read books where the quiet, sensitive, intelligent heroine finds refuge among rows of words. Except I am not particularly quiet and not half as clever as I think I am. I am thick-fringed, chatty, keen to please with the potential to be a little pain in the backside. I am not here because this library has been my refuge for years. I am here because I am the new girl, again, and in mapping uncharted territory, the library—any library—is my North Star, my first port of call for finding my way.

I do love words though.

I may not have the telekinesis of Matilda but that at least is something we share. Moving across different country and classroom borders, I've noticed words. The way you say them packs a punch in the playground. The way someone's eyes crinkle when you catch them unexpectedly with a joke. Plus, no matter how unfamiliar the faces, almost every library has a copies of the *Harry Potter* books. I am lucky that the countries Dad's job has posted us to all share English, which soon becomes my favourite subject.

There are word patterns, too, in first days, the way well-meaning teachers make introductions and implorations to bored looking students while I cringe.

'This is Amanda, she's come over from Singapore.'

'This is Amanda. Her family has just moved here from London.'

'This is Amanda. She's moved back to the UK from Australia.'

'Please make her feel welcome.'

One day, when I'm thirteen, a girl called Charlotte takes the teacher at her word and fishes me out of piles of Terry Pratchett to ask if I want to have lunch with her and her friends. She is pretty and kind and funny in a gentle sort of way, and without a second thought, I close the pages on the Discworld and shut the door on my old friends.

I still speak to Char now. She's a doctor and her three little girls have her blonde hair and wide smile and quiet instinct for kindness.

After Char plucks me from the library, I still love words but I learn to use them in different ways. I use them to make people laugh. I use them to argue. Char, Bry, Anna Rosanna, and I attempt to form a band, and I use them for a while to write very bad indie lyrics. Later, I use them in bars, to flirt for an extra drink, thinking as the short Asian woman, I'll need to rely on my banter instead of my looks. I use them in my media jobs, to interview, to write articles, to persuade people to speak at conferences and share their own words.

I become a journalist. It seems the obvious career choice for someone who loves words though I soon learn that loving words is only part of the equation. I learn words can be dangerous. I watch colleagues pore for hours over one sentence, fretting over the choice of words. Are they misleading, too flowery, too sparse? Will they get us into trouble? And do we care?

I learn that words are only a tool for the most important thing, which is the truth. This is an unfashionable and untrendy mantra for many journalists now, but those who believe it believe it hard.

I report on activists' angry protests bouncing off state buildings as we obliterate the planet. Books with chapters and songs with lyrics that break hearts across borders. Love declared through sonnets, or even sometimes, a text.

Maybe, I think, temporarily bloated with the power of the page, we're all closer to Matilda than I thought. Maybe it is a sort of magic.

Or maybe it's just markings on paper, all talk, no action. Maybe, sometimes, they're the same thing.

A Heartlands Girl

Chua Mui Hoong grew up in Singapore's heartlands, in a traditional kampung *attap* house, named after the leaves used to thatch the roof. Then she moved to a one-room public housing HDB flat, then a three-room, where she, her siblings, and her parents 'spent many happy, tumultuous years living cheek by jowl'.

She's slept in wood-panelled rooms and attended formal dinners abroad. She's lived in private condominiums in fashionable suburbs, and small cramped rooms. As a former political columnist and opinion editor at Singapore's dominant broadsheet *The Straits Times*, she delved into issues of social inequality and change, themes she carried through in her most recent book, *Singapore, Disrupted.*

I reach out to Chua because she is a living breathing example of the social mobility the Lion City proudly touts: a heartlands girl who's risen up the ranks of white-collar professionalism. Some of the city-state's most prominent civil servants have similar stories. Education minister Chan Chun Sing is the son of a single mother who straddled two jobs, working as a cleaner in the day and as a machine-operator in a factory at night. Senior Minister of State for Sustainability and the Environment Amy Khor would conduct delivery dashes around her school, selling her mother's popular Chinese desserts to schoolteachers[36] at a jacked-up price to meet sweet-toothed demand.

The first thing Chua does when we catch up over Zoom is question the concept of Singaporean class altogether.

'There's so much baggage in that term,' she says. 'And it often comes from a specific way of looking at society in terms of social strata. In Singapore, when we speak of social divisions, we tend to speak in terms of economic status and maybe lifestyles. I think, in the European context, class has a lot more going for it. There's association with family culture, your political beliefs.'

Chua's parents emigrated from Shantou to Singapore in the decades before Independence. At first, they worked odd jobs—carpentry, hauling bricks—to pay for their rented room. Later, they bought a trishaw with a $50 lottery windfall and turned to selling local snacks and dishes to support their three children.

Her classmates were children of noodle-sellers, cleaners, teachers, and bankers. It wasn't until she won a government scholarship to Cambridge University in the UK, among students whose parents warned them about gold-digging girlfriends, that she first became aware of class as something entrenched in history, with barriers you shouldn't cross. 'It was a jarring realization of being working class in a highly privileged and quite foreign environment,' she remembers.

For Chua, born in the first decade of Singapore's independence, the untapped potential of her generation aligned with the untapped potential of a newly-fledged country establishing its identity.

While there were still social disparities under this new Singapore, Chua remembers inequality based more around race than family income. Colonial times saw an established racial pecking order, with the British firmly on top and the Malays holding a certain social status due to the Sultanate's role in negotiating power over to Stamford Raffles. After Independence, she says, 'The Chinese as the majority were catapulted to the top of socio-economic structure.' Still, she insists that the playing field was overall level and open to anyone.

Now that her generation of 'working class upstarts' has children and grandchildren of their own, Chua has noticed changes, both in education and elitism. Exams, which she views as 'one of the only truly merit based means of assessment' have become intensively pressurized, causing a mental health crisis across schools. On average, anxiety and depression cost a Singaporean student around twenty-four days off school every year.[37] Chua blames her own generation, 'middle-aged parents who are repeating [what] they were taught about striving . . . that has bred a culture of hyper-competition that is very unhealthy for us as a society.'

There's also a growing focus on networks. Not just where you went to school, but where your parents went to school, whose fathers were friends or business partners. According to Chua, it comes accompanied by a quiet unforgiving judgement that's replaced the 'willingness to look beyond whatever might be socially jarring behaviour . . . to recognize the talent in that person', which she remembers from her early professional years.

This is starting to reflect the very 'western', concept of class that Chua was so keen to dispel at the beginning of our conversation. The centuries-old social preconceptions seeped into our culture like an old stain in a sofa. Maybe this is an unhappy by-product of progress. The longer your development journey, the more class baggage you accumulate.

Disruption is the only thing that pulls a switch on the tracks. Those best placed to drive it, according to Chua, are those who bridge the ever-shifting divide between 'outsider' and 'insider'. Those who've crossed the dividing lines between social classes but still keep one foot on the ground of their upbringing, manoeuvring skilfully as the gaps grow and the turfs shift apart slowly.

'When it comes to intergenerational social connections, someone like me is a complete outsider,' she points out. '[But] I am an insider because I am a part and beneficiary of the Singapore government scholarship system and civil service leaders are people I went to university with.'

Social mobility may have opened doors to the elite, but Chua prefers to stay firmly on the threshold, looking in, a skill not taught in any classroom, but learned over a lifetime. 'As a journalist, I maintain that outsider perspective,' she says. 'I try to critique the system I benefitted from and be a voice for those who are even more outsider than I am. It's quite a discomfiting position. But I think it's an incredibly enriching one.'

How Do We Work?

Everyone is busy in Singapore. The harried office workers walking in flocks through the central business district. The old uncles and aunties carting racks of tightly pressed discarded cardboard. The bearded hipsters crouched over their iPads, slurping on iced matcha lattes using coffee shop Wi-Fi. The migrant construction workers dangling from cranes to put the finishing touches on slinky condominiums with home offices. Many people we meet have two jobs, one to pay the bills and a passion project side hustle. Singapore has an unemployment rate of 2.76 per cent,[38] well under the global average of around 5.1 per cent.[39] People are here to work.

Paul and I have come here to work as well. Behind all the existential talk about figuring out who we are is a solid job offer. Paul's international law firm transferred him to their Singapore team. I got a job at an international media company, then at a regional features magazine covering news across Southeast Asia. We are here to join the sea of the gainfully employed.

Maybe it's the immigrant mentality in me, but work was always a core part of our home life, a constant, no matter which country we were in. Work was the long hours that kept my dad at the office. Work was the mentality of 'never be idle', that you could do anything you want as long as you were always doing something.

Work was part of my identity and, when I felt I was good at it, it was the biggest high I'd ever felt. When I felt like I was failing, the lows were crushing.

Searching for personal fulfilment in work is a relatively modern phenomenon. But it goes further than scratching fragile egos. Singapore's founding father Lee Kuan Yew said it himself, 'There must be no fooling around, work means discipline. Singapore's success depends on the spirit in which workers, management and government . . . enter into the spirit of cooperation necessary for prosperity.'[40] Work, then, was not as an individual but as part of a whole, part of something bigger.

We don't always get up because we feel it's going to be a great day. We get up for a purpose. Families need feeding, bills need paying, a living needs to be made. A series of small obligations pushes us from one day to the next. Sometimes that purpose is bigger—work as part of a larger nation, a collective effort. Who are we without this purpose? Are we brave enough to find out?

'We need to talk,' says my CEO.

There have been rumblings in the sector for a while. The threateningly efficient advent of AI. The shakedown of local independent newsrooms in the region. Voice of Democracy in Cambodia closed suddenly after then-prime minister Hun Sen took issue with how an article portrayed his son. Vice Media APAC announced mass layoffs amid global restructuring.

Uncertainty spread through local media like a virus, wages were delayed, reporters living pay cheque to pay cheque relied on friends and managers to lend them money for rent. Our newsroom winds down its editorial operations at the end of a mercilessly hot September.

For the first time in decades I am unemployed. 'Funemployed', as people call it, people who've assumedly never had to worry about the next month's salary or who've struggled with basing their identity around their career.

I ride the metro at strange times, with fellow strange hour companions. Grandparents fussing over fractious grandchildren. University students plugged into casket headphones and TikTok. The occasional lone man in army combats, heading home for leave, his surname stitched to the front of his army shirt.

I explore new places. A Chinese Garden with a white and fiery orange pagoda reflected in the waters of a glassy lake. A Japanese garden, where a coral red bridge arches between banks of scholars' rocks and stone temples. I go to a Nanyin concert, Southern Chinese court music with roots in the Han dynasty's palace court, a million miles away from the Brit pop and indie rock that louchely wheedle their way into my playlists. The reedy *dongxiao* bamboo flute and the double voice of the two-string *erxian* fiddle sing a story about a sign maker who emigrated from China at the turn of the twentieth century, another story of a new start in Singapore.

I learn to knit. I start to learn Mandarin again. I watch a lot of Netflix. I drink a lot of wine. After a few weeks, I throw myself back into the job market, flooding recruiters' inboxes, reaching out to networks, ready once again to sell myself.

I have learned a few new things during my funemployment and something about myself, which is that maybe I'm not brave enough yet to figure out who I am when I'm not doing something, when I'm not being someone.

It is the weekend. The city centre is sleepy and hungover; the street corners near the closed bars smell of stale beer and good memories. Paul and I take a metro out east to Ang Mo Kio. We walk through the open lobbies of HDB blocks to a vast stretch of green, where tall shadowy poles shoot from the ground like saplings. But these aren't trees. At the top of each pole's curved hook hangs a bulbous cage. Each one houses a tenant, a bristling mass of feathers, a pair of sharp curved claws.

The Kebun Baru Birdsinging Club is one of the largest in Southeast Asia. It's a social gathering where old and young men gather in weekend groups around the nearby arena to rate theirs and other birds in categories including pitch, plumage, frequency, and the elusive 'beauty of melody'. It's a hobby and a passion, one that can come with a hefty price tag. A prized songbird can fetch tens of thousands of dollars.

The pastime has become such an important part of local leisure life that songbird rearing became part of the country's National Heritage Board list of Intangible Cultural Heritage in 2018.

Songbirds are social creatures. They'll generally only sing when other birds of the same species are around. The ones at the top of the hanging poles aren't in competition but their sound still stretches thinly across the grass in brief tangled verses amid tripping melodies. They are separated but together. Caged but singing freely. Playful and productive, reminding us how what we do is both small and significant, and sometimes is for no reason at all.

SOFT WHITE UNDERBELLY

Locked Down

Someone is sick in China. It started when a virus being tested in a high security lab in south China's Wuhan suffered a leak. No, wait, it started when a Wuhan resident chewed off the head of a bat and gnawed its bloody body, ingesting something that was going to severely disagree with them. Actually, hold on, it started when a Chinaman fucked a pangolin, a pretty impressive feat, given the scales on the thing.

Either way, something happened in China, and now people's lungs are shutting down and so are countries.

The World Health Organization becomes the world's new daily weather forecast. PM Lee makes an announcement via Facebook live. There is a four-day warning before the country shuts down; time to rush to the supermarkets and stock up for the impending apocalypse.

Paul and I divide and conquer. I come home stocked with chocolate chip cookies, flapjacks, Earl Grey tea. Paul returns with pasta, cereal, and toilet paper. I'm glad we're married. It's clear which one of us would be a goner first in a real apocalypse situation.

In the checkout queue, you see people exposed. Young mothers bulk buying powder milk. An old lady buying a tiny frying pan for a single egg.

Our experience of the pandemic is a Groundhog Day shared across the world. Hours spill hazily into each other like colouring outside the lines. We doomscroll the news and numbly process case numbers and death tolls like weather reports. Pub quizzes and baby showers behind glitching laptop screens. We are the lucky ones, our jobs allow us to work from the cushy confines of our flat. Your money or your life is a cliché, but for many frontline and front-facing workers, the pandemic made it a grim reality.

We mark our fourth anniversary with a takeaway pizza and a celebratory appetizer, a fat blob of burrata that wobbles in its plastic box like a dollop of tippex.

But outside, the virus continues to spread. It spreads despite the masks and the wheezing pumps of hand sanitizer bottles. It spreads like rumours and worrying statistics that smear themselves across every digital surface.

The world enters an Olympic race for vaccines. We file into community centres to get jabbed and poked by expressionless volunteers. We each collect a free box of face masks as we leave. I attend my first Zoom wedding. I attend my first Zoom funeral.

There are occasional grumblings around this see-saw control on socializing. A two-person limit on gatherings for a four-person family splits parents and kids across tables. The understanding is that it's for the greater good. To protect especially the senior demographic of Singapore's ageing population, who are more vulnerable to the virus and who are more likely to be suspicious of vaccines, shunning western drugs for the familiarity of traditional Chinese medicine.

A front-page headline is run on a ninety-year-old woman's death from the virus, and uncomfortable debates are mumbled across socially-distanced rooms. Is one old person dying a headline? How much do we sacrifice to try and prevent the inevitable?

In brighter news, there is a rap—a viral comedy skit with a contagiously catchy beat by Singaporean comedy icons Phua Chu Kang and Irene Ang—called 'Get Your Shot, Steady Pom Pi Pi'. It's Singlish for someone who's able to hold it together in chaotic times. I watch it obsessively then, because I'm a good moral citizen, and I don't have much to do, I send it to everyone on my contact list. Who says things can't spread under lockdown?

Mel, separated from her partner Wil in Hong Kong for over a year, becomes an expertly obsessive home smoothie maker. Jason from Beng Who Cooks launches a foundation Beng Who Cares, providing free meals to anyone struggling in the Covid-hit economy.

Then, slowly, surely, cases taper out. Singapore shuffles the number of people allowed to hang out together like a teacher controlling a class of naughty schoolchildren, from five to two, to eight. We each collect a cute dinky token from the nearest community centre, which logs our every entry and exit point, our own personal germ-tracker Tamagotchi.

By April 2022, things reopen for good. Clarke Quay pulses with the bass beats of reopened nightclubs, like a cardiac patient resuscitated at the last moment. The world goes back to normal, shoving a 'new' in front of it like a promotional bargain.

We attend Ah Beng's leaving party, where we down sambuca shots while his pet tortoise Little Beng shuffles in his tank on the bar. A two-year business hiatus followed by spiking rent prices has made being food's bad boy turned good unaffordable in Duxton. (He'll later, after a stint at a sandwich joint called Wild Crumbs, come back fighting with a resurrected Beng Who Cooks on the East Coast.)

Singapore was deemed, by a *Bloomberg* resilience report, to be one of the best places to be during the pandemic and maintained one of the lowest death tolls worldwide.[41] But under that, there are the inconvenient truths, the ugly side to the success story. The fact that a crisis brings out the worst in us as much as it brings out the best in us. That we all fall, but some of us fall further and harder and without a safety net and are kept down by others and their fear. That we've spent the last few years together. But we've also spent them alone.

Forgotten Cases

Over 90 per cent of Singapore's reported 60,000 Covid cases are across the migrant worker community by April 2021.[42]

Singapore is a city built by migrants. The approximately 1.2 million migrant workers currently in Singapore make up around 38 per cent of the workforce. Hailing primarily from Bangladesh, India, and China, they work predominantly in the country's low-wage sectors: domestic work, marine repair, and construction.

You see them packed into open-air trucks at the end of their shifts, squatting on plastic chairs with the legs lopped off as they're ferried from construction sites to dormitories on the outskirts of the city. You see them sleeping off the heat in the shade of a bridge in the short break between shifts. You see them dangling like marionettes from harnesses as they work on the city's ever-growing high-rises. But they're mostly in the background, a comfortable side note to the national narrative of rapid progress.

The pandemic shuts Singapore's migrant workers away and makes them more visible than they'd been in years. Stories of Covid tearing through tightly-packed, unsanitary dormitory blocks where hundreds of thousands of migrant workers live stacked like empty pizza boxes, alongside reports of rising numbers of suicides and attempted suicides, seep into the news.[43]

'What's going on in Singapore?' friends message from abroad. We are hitting the international headlines for all the wrong reasons.

We're technically foreign workers too. My grandparents, my parents, even Paul and I, crossing borders in search of jobs, money, better opportunities. It's a well-trodden migrant path.

But unlike the occupants of these crowded dorms, I have always felt seen, almost too visible. The awkward new girl. The happy red-wine flushed faces of our white neighbours at our Lunar New Year reunion dinner as they played poker and twirled prosperity noodles around chopsticks like spaghetti. A friend's earnest question when complaining about her Chinese boss. 'Is it, like, a cultural thing?'

What cushy middle-class threshold divides 'different types of immigrants'? From the type you snipe about in opinion columns and social media sound bites for taking your jobs to those silently doing the jobs you don't want to do? What's the dividing line between awkward scrutiny, each difference exaggerated, and being swept under the social carpet?

The migrant workers' housing crisis is described by Nominated Member of Parliament, Associate Professor Walter Theseira, as a 'humanitarian disaster' in 2020.[44] There are counterarguments. Employers would yelp at the increased cost of improving dormitory conditions, they say. The Foreign Employee Dormitory Act regulations had never been drafted to consider something as wide-scale and unexpected as the pandemic. We can't make changes in the heart of a crisis. Let's get through the heat of the virus first, then address the issue.

That year the government announces the introduction of new 'Quick Build Dormitories'. Later, standards are set for improved living conditions, such as ensuite toilets and a cap of twelve people to a bedroom.[45] But many migrant workers were still confined to one cramped room for almost twenty-four hours a day.

As the rest of the world trudges towards a 'new normal', in the dorms, things stay mostly the same. Of the approximately 280,000 workers who live in dormitories, a maximum of 25,000 are permitted to travel outside the designated recreation centres near their dorms or their workplaces on weekdays, only with an authorized 'exit pass' from the government and for a time limit of eight hours.[46] On the weekends, this rises to 50,000.

In June 2022, the exit passes are replaced with a 'popular places pass', limiting migrant workers to just four of their most popular haunts: Chinatown, Little India, Jurong East, and Geylang Serai. This bubbles along like Long Covid until the end of 2022, when it fades dormant into the background.

During the height of the health crisis, a book is published by Alex Au, an activist and vice-president of transient workers charitable organization TWC2, called *The Trouble with Foreign Workers*.

In it, Au claims that the overcrowded beds and poor ventilation were not the problem. Instead, they were a symptom of an underlying rot, an 'addiction to cheap labour . . . an economic model that is reliant on these workers for our prosperity . . . we seem to fear that if we don't keep them cheap, then we Singaporeans will miss out.'

The migrant workers seem to agree with him, at least when it comes to the housing part. Pre-Covid surveys found that in general, migrants tended not to complain about their dorms. Some had positive feedback, some had negative. Most were just resigned. They were much more preoccupied with non-payment of salary, unpaid medical leave, lack of overtime pay, exorbitant relocation agents fees, and payments demanded for work permits.

Still, the image of a dirty crowded sleeping area has become a thumbnail for the entire male migrant experience in the Red Dot. It's a shortcut to claim we understand these background figures, connected to their home countries by umbilical cords in the remittance centres and money transfer kiosks lining the pavements in Singapore's backstreets.

It's easy to put people in a box like this, almost as easy as it is to stack them into rows of bunk beds lining grubby walls like supermarket shelves. It's easy to view the housing conditions and the social isolation as the root cause rather than symptoms of an underlying illness in a society. It allows for quick fixes, band-aids to patch the problem.

Three years after the start of the pandemic, in September 2023, the Ministry of Manpower's 'Proof of Acceptable Accommodation' requirements for migrant worker employers in three sectors—Construction, Marine Shipyard and Process (CMP)—are introduced, a move praised by advocacy groups as a 'step in the right direction'.

Migrant workers re-fade into the background. They'll stay there until the next issue arises, propelling them into the news again, spreading suspicion and sympathy until we slowly become immune.

Hassan

I meet Hassan in his bedroom, which is also his living area, which is also the office of TWC2. There is a camp bed pressed against a wall, with a towel hanging over a fold-out chair. Under it, there is a football.

Hassan himself is perched on the chair, in his well-fitting football shirt. He has large caramel-coloured eyes under a mop of bouncy black curls. He looks a bit like a former teen model, someone who's used to owning the room, even when that room is a stuffy, sparse office with only two audience members: me and a bored looking man who introduced himself as 'Hassan's brother', and then submerged himself into his iPhone.

Propped against Hassan's chair leg, by his white sneakers, is a pair of bulky plastic crutches.

In a city where migrant workers are the invisible cogs that power the slick metropolitan machine, Hassan is what happens when there is a glitch. After working for a Chinese steel fabricator for almost a decade, the twenty-seven-year-old was in the middle of a ten-hour shift when the piece of metal he was welding slipped and crushed his leg, causing him to fall awkwardly and tear a ligament. Long waiting times for an operation have put him out of work for over a year. 'In Singapore, the bosses need to earn, they don't care about you, how you makan [eat], your housing, your treatment. It is very bad if you have an accident,' he says, tilting back slightly and fixing me with a pointed look.

Since then, he's been living in a limbo. Under the Ministry of Manpower (MOM)'s Employment Act, migrant workers are entitled to overtime, annual rest days, and sick leave, including paid hospitalization leave. But when Hassan was injured, his company revoked his work pass entirely.

Workplace injuries aren't uncommon among male migrant workers. The long shifts, tight deadlines, and hard physical labour in sectors that dominate their employment create a perfect storm of high injury risk. Local news is seasoned with the occasional headline like the ones on foreign Bangladeshi workers killed by falling pipes or struck by a steel frame.[47]

Hassan's brother is no actual relation, but a fellow Bangladeshi worker called Hossain. While Hossain was drilling on-site, a piece of cement ricocheted under his protective goggles and lodged itself in his pupil. An operation later and his sight is saved, but his work visa is revoked, and with it the main reason he is here in Singapore: to send money back to his family in Bangladesh. 'I come to Singapore to send money to my family,' he says darkly. 'Now, three months, I give no money, not even one dollar. My family has many problems coming . . .'

I am left on this cliffhanger. Hassan and Hossain are also on a cliffhanger, a somewhat more serious one, as they shuttle back and forth between home and the Ministry of Manpower to get short term permissions to stay in the country, in limbo between two lives and two countries.

'Are you married?' Hassan asks suddenly. I tell him I am. He looks serious. He was seeing a woman back in Bangladesh before he came to Singapore. 'She was my first real relationship. But it didn't work out,' he says. Years later he finds himself still thinking about her occasionally and struggling to find new romance in the frenetic Lion City. He fixes me with a knowing, worldly-wise look and says, 'To be with a migrant worker . . . you need a good head.'

This isn't how I imagined this interview to go. Relationship advice is an unexpected detour in my amateur exploration into Singapore's social issues. But at our core, we're all anchored to the search for the same things—family, belonging, love—no matter our circumstances or how far we are from home. I ask if his ex ever considered moving over to Singapore with him.

It isn't that simple. A job as a man in Singapore is, Hassan states confidently, 'not hard to get'. The sectors that attract a lot of male migrant labour have quotas capped at around 10–18 per cent of a company's workforce on the number of foreign S-Pass visas they can hand out, but the bar to entry is generally low. Women, who tend to be restricted to jobs as foreign domestic workers, are subject to a host of MOM requirements. They have to be the right age (between twenty-three and fifty), come from the right country,[48] and have a minimum eight years of formal education.

If they jump through these hoops, there is the question of personal intimacy: sharing a home, not with colleagues around your own age and background, but with a family with their own connections, histories, breakfast routines. You swap raising your own children for a stranger's, sometimes forming bonds that rival the ones you have back home.

So, yes, you need a 'good head' as Hassan suggests. As a Bangladeshi woman, you need a good head to calculate the sacrifices you are prepared to make. Do you risk your children becoming distant while you raise someone else's, so you can feed their future? Or fall in love with someone to live parallel lives while he risks his life building a city of someone else's ambitions?

'Leaving Bangladesh, it doesn't just affect the people in Bangladesh,' Hassan says sagely. 'Women wait and wait, then they get tired of waiting.' He nods at the sparse room around him. 'All the men I work with, I say, 90 per cent it happens to them like this.'

I ask the question that's been preying on my mind. With the hardship, the heartache, the limbs, the eyes, the agency fees, and the precarious job security, do they regret the move?

In some ways, this is an obvious question. It's obvious because the past few years have seen Bangladesh topple from a rising star of economic development, fuelled by the large youth population, to a country caught in the crossfire of political and economic tensions. In March and April 2020, 61.57 per cent of people lost their jobs due to the pandemic.[49] Together with rising inflation and foreign debt, these factors have been fanning the flames of resentful protesters in the country.

Or, more simply, as Hassan puts it, 'I stay in Bangladesh, I study for a degree, then a Masters, then maybe I survive to become a rickshaw driver.'

It is an obvious question because both men, like almost all their peers, have put themselves into thousands of dollars of agency debt to take a gamble on a new Singaporean life. Or, as Hossain says, 'When I paid 7,000

Singapore [dollars] to my [relocation] agent, I think I am coming [for] one year working, two year[s] working, I pay back, I go back to my family, Now I [am] injured, I go back to Bangladesh, I die. [They] will catch me.'

But there is something else too. There is a pride over a new identity, one formed by a communal resilience, an ability to work anywhere, to make it through whatever tough situations this foreign country might throw at you. This is what it means to be an immigrant. This is what it means to be Bangladeshi. It's estimated that the diaspora is one of the largest in the world, with around 7.5 million living outside their home country.[50]

'Everywhere you can find Bangla men,' nods Hossain, sounding uncharacteristically cheerful. 'Us Banglas . . . we are everywhere!'

As Hassan hobbles to see me out, I ask him if he misses Bangladesh, if he wants to come home. He flashes me a wide, white, movie star smile. 'My mum is always asking,' he shrugs. 'She says, "Come home! Get married!" I tell her "Give me time! I am not done here yet. I am not ready."'

Remembering the Riots

8 December 2013

As his Sunday rest day drew to a close on 8 December 2013, Sakthivel Kumaravelu boarded the private bus that ferried workers from Singapore's Little India to their dormitory in Jalan Papan on the western outskirts of the city. Tipsy and fractious from an afternoon fuelled by the café-bars and liquor shops around the area, he was asked to dismount after he allegedly dropped his Bermuda shorts in the aisle.

As the doors closed and the bus drove off without him, the thirty-three-year-old construction worker sprinted down the rain-soaked streets, brandishing an umbrella at the fast-receding tail lights. It paused at Race Course Road, and Kumaravelu tried to mount the bus. He missed and fell.

Around forty minutes later, his crushed body was extricated by police officers.

Within minutes, Kumaravelu's death had lit a fuse. Onlookers spread the word and soon around 400 members of the country's migrant community flooded the streets in furious protest. Ten days before International Migrants Day, various dialects mixed with the sound of splintering glass as the streets of Little India glowed orange with the searing heat of burning cars. The rioters chanted 'Kill the woman, burn the bus,' targeting and attacking the driver Lee Kim Huat and bus timekeeper Grace Wong Geck Woon after rumours spread that she had pushed Kumaravelu off the bus.

The Little India Riots injured sixty-two people and went down in history as Singapore's worst case of public violence in decades.

8 December 2022

It is a muggy grey day and a heavy anniversary. Back in London, the air has turned crisp and cold and the supermarkets bleed festive red with offers on mince pies and goose-pimpled turkeys. But here, despite the ornate lights and sparkling Christmas trees piercing through the warm evening air on

Orchard Road, people aren't full swing into Christmas yet. We've only just finished Deepavali and, in between these two festive celebrations, I'm at Little India to mark a different occasion: the night when, nine years ago, a drunk Indian labourer fell under the wheels of a bus.

On that day, A.K.M Mohsin heard the shouting and police sirens from his office in the Bangladeshi Workers' Centre on Rowell Road. The walls are warm cornflower blue and on one of them hangs a framed copy of *Banglar Kantha,* the country's only Bengali-language newspaper, which he set up in 2006, after moving to Singapore in 1991. That night, the centre was a hub of noise. On weekends, Mohsin used the centre as a space to organize social and cultural activities for the city's roughly 150,000 strong Bangladeshi migrant community. There were the sounds of a play being rehearsed, lines from a song being practised for an upcoming competition.

'Then a group ran upstairs and told me that something was going on in the Tekka [area],' Mohsin says. 'At around ten or eleven, someone else came up and said he'd heard someone had been killed, that they'd died in a road accident. No one really knew what was going on.'

He walked through the rain until he reached the site of the accident. By that time, it was almost midnight and the rioters had mostly dispersed. Mohsin was met by a gaggle of police officers and debris. He made a call to a contact at the Bangladesh High Commission before he saw the news report confirming that Kumaravelu was Indian not Bangladeshi. 'The first thing I thought was that this will be very dangerous for the migrant community overall,' he remembers. 'And very bad for our job security.'

Fifty-six-year-old Mohsin has been working with Singapore's migrant communities for almost twenty years. He has been working with the Bangladesh Centre since 2005, and in 2011, set up Dibashram, a cultural space for Bangladeshi migrants to come together through poetry, theatre, and other arts-based groups. Alongside this, he campaigns to improve conditions and rights for a group he says, 'continues to be exploited by their employers and business'. He points to the fact that some dorms aren't equipped for their residents to cook their own meals. The third-party vendors hired by caterers, including unregistered providers, have reportedly left bags of cooked food, packed in Styrofoam boxes, unattended and exposed.[51] He recounts conversations he's had with government departments about the open-air lorries, plastic chairs with the legs lopped off, ferrying awkwardly squatting men between their shifts by the truckload. 'It's not safe and not nice also,' he says. 'When I spoke to the Ministry of Manpower people, I said, "My country is a very poor country. And we do not even transport humans like that."'

Overall, he says, he's found the government receptive in these conversations; the main challenge lies with the minority of unregulated private companies 'who just want to make a quick profit'.

But in the aftermath of the Little India Riots, he saw new, restricting levels of damage control.

A Committee of Inquiry (COI) was set up. Fifty-seven migrant workers deported and banned permanently from Singapore. A further 213 were issued warnings and briefed on Singapore's laws and zero-tolerance policy on rioting. Intoxication was blamed as a contributing factor for both Kumaravelu's fall and the ensuing violence.[52] Over a year later, the 2015 Liquor Control Act marked Little India and nearby Geylang as designated 'Liquor Control Zones', and prohibited the public consumption of alcohol from 10.30 p.m. to 7 a.m. in all public places every day.

For a period of about a year afterwards, Mohsin recalls, migrants were banned from entering the Little India zone. 'All the remittance centres were based in the Little India area,' he explains. 'They don't come, how do they send money to their families? There was a lot of stress at that time.' Remittance centres were later set up nearer the dormitories; monetary veins connecting residents to their home countries, giving them one less reason to leave these self-contained enclaves, further increasing the distance between 'us' and 'them'.

Singapore has an uneasy history with riots. The clashes of 1964 and 1969 were flashpoints of an earlier uneasy merger between Singapore and Malaysia and a boiling point of tensions between the ethnic Malay and Chinese communities, which contributed to the rupture between the two countries.

These riots are often described as 'race riots'. Maybe that's why it's easy to sometimes also colour discussions of the Little India Riots with tinges of race—triggered by an altercation between an Indian and Chinese man—despite the fact that some of the harshest critics of the riots I've spoken to have been Indian Singaporeans.

My mum remembers the sound of her plastic *kuti kuti* tokens clacking against the pavement like nervous fingernails in 1964. She played round after round with her cousin John, hour after hour, until the sound was drowned out by the sirens calling them in for curfew. She was seven years old.

Schools started emergency preparation training and sent a letter home requesting students to bring extra food in case they got trapped in the building. My mum started an underground market, trading her dry Marie water biscuits and tins of spam for more interesting trinkets.

She remembers the stories, whispered through the neat straight roads of her Holland Village neighbourhood. A motorcyclist speeding down Kallang Pudding Road hadn't seen the wire stretched taut across the road and had driven straight into it. A Malay trishaw rider was making his rounds through Geylang. His three-wheeled carriage shuddered as he bumped down the uneven pavement, cycling straight into the sharp blade of a pointed knife.

One day, her father came home with a surprise. It looked like a box, a black frame around a square screen that bulged slightly like a glass eye. A television! After that, afternoons under curfew were less dull. There were cartoons, interrupted by news updates of dancing flames from empty windows, glittery shards of glass flying, stone-eyed faces ugly under puffy bandages, all looking strangely mystical in monochrome.

By the end of July, she had fifty multicoloured kuti kuti tokens, the most out of all the kids in the neighbourhood. The riots had left twenty-three people dead and 454 injured.[53]

It's easy to focus on the divide between 'us' and the 'foreigners'; the peaceful, well-structured country, which has maintained social order for decades, against the unruliness of, what Mohsin half-seriously refers to as, the 'Bangladesh' or 'India' way, storming the streets and causing havoc. But I worry this bypasses the real issues. The continuing news stories of migrant workers injured—sometimes fatally—at work.[54] The tendency to forget that uprooting yourself to go to an unfamiliar country is generally a push more than a pull situation, to view migrant communities as a group, glossing over the individual stories of why they're here, why they had to leave.

Mohsin has his own migrant story. His father, Abdul Malek Bhuiyan, was a pioneer and branch founder of Bangladesh's oldest political party, the Awami League, and a prominent grassroots activist and leader in the uprising against the military in the 1971 Liberation War. Growing up, he watched Bhuiyan immersed in their country's fight for independence.

'I was only seven or eight years old,' he recalls. 'But I still saw how much my father struggled.' Years later, when the 1990 mass uprising spread through the student community, the young Mohsin joined the demonstrations. He was arrested and jailed for a month. 'The prison was just across the street from my house,' he says with a small smile. 'I could see it from the cell window. I wouldn't eat the prison food, so my family would walk down the street and deliver me meals.'

That's all he'll say on the subject.

After his release, Mohsin's family decided that it would be better for him to continue his studies abroad. Singapore stood out as somewhere near, somewhere safe, and somewhere familiar with a large Bangladeshi community. That was thirty-one years ago. Since then, he has married and moved his wife over to join him in the Lion City. They've had three children, all born in Singapore. They've taken on Permanent Resident status. Singaporeans, he says, have overall been warm and welcoming. They've helped make the country feel like home. I ask him if he'd consider citizenship. It seems the natural next step. But Mohsin shakes his head.

'After everything my father did and everything I saw him go through, I couldn't give up my [Bangladesh] citizenship,' he says. 'I still belong to that country. And I still owe it to him.'

An Evening in Geylang

7 p.m.

Drugs are strictly illegal in Singapore, but someone hasn't told the cockroaches. A pair of them are tangoing dizzily in a gutter, having sipped from the rim of a discarded codeine bottle. 'They're high,' says Yizhou, nodding cheerfully at their locked antennae. 'They might make love. Or rip each other's faces off.'

Geylang is the red light district and vice capital of Singapore. In a city so squeaky clean even chewing gum is banned, all the subterfuge bubbles together in one tightly concentrated melting pot of sin. There are syringes on the ground and cameras clinging to the lampposts in Geylang. Coincidentally, the place also has glowing recommendations for some of the best durian and frog leg porridge on the main island, but I'm sure that's just an unrelated bonus.

The area is also Yinzhou's neighbourhood. He started Geylang Adventures as a school project running 'secret tours' around his childhood beat. Now, it's a not-so-secret side hustle with its own logo, which sits bright against his jet-black T-shirt, a Frankenstein's monster of half-spiky durian shell, half-seductive crimson lantern. 'The two things Geylang is known for,' he says cheerfully. 'Good food and prostitution!'

Yinzhou throws social titbits like breadcrumbs as we wind our way through the back alleys and walk through busy streets that were once plantations run by a rich Arab family selling lemongrass for soap and rheumatism medication in the nineteenth century.

'We're just turning past the church here. Geylang has the highest concentration of brothels in Singapore, but also the highest concentration of religious institutions. A real mix of salvation and sin!

'Look at these old shophouses. You see the spiral staircases winding down the exterior? These were used by the night soil collectors. They'd come and collect all the human waste from your house at night. We had night soil collectors in Singapore until the eighties.'

Most cities have a Geylang. We dress it up in sexy bad-boy euphemisms like 'the rough side of town'. We cover it up like human excrement collectors under the comfortable darkness of night. We're both repulsed by it and fascinated by it, like a tangoing cockroach, uncertain whether to tear it down or fetishize its griminess.

'People come for the brothels,' says Yinzhou cheerfully. 'But they come back for the durians.'

8 p.m.

Pop-up street vendors stand outside the fish and fruit markets, selling their own range of wares to help consumers . . . pop up. Dull, opal blue diamonds of viagra. Boxes of the Malaysian herbal remedy *tongkat ali*, known for its uplifting qualities.

Drugs are a tetchy subject in Singapore. Possession or consumption of cannabis can cost you up to thirty years in prison and strokes of the cane.[55] Trafficking can cost you your life. But the cockroaches aren't the only ones getting high. There are parties in hotel rooms where groups of Canadian and American expats snack on smuggled packs of jewel-bright gummy bears laced with LSD. There are house parties I hear about where students get giggly on the boxes of weed they're growing on the sills of their student housing.

There are the people who've left the discarded syringes, who buy the pills and small crystalline packets from online messaging apps or these streetside makeshift tables. According to Yinzhou, the government knows that this illicit activity is happening in Geylang but, overall, containment seems to be better than the risk of sin seeping into other areas of the city.

Once in a while, there'll be a high-profile raid. Officers will seize huge amounts of ecstasy, cannabis, ketamine, and a couple of dealers hiding in a Geylang hotel room. Reports of 'crackdowns' and 'drug busts' will make the headlines.[56] The world will move on.

8.30 p.m.

We move onto an open-air alley, just out of sight of the 'twitchers', the orb-shaped cameras watching over the streets. They've been there in increased numbers in areas with high migrant numbers since the Little India riots and track for potential new disturbances through high-tech monitors of body heat and concentration. The alley used to be the site of Singapore's largest open-air, unlicensed gambling den, before law enforcement stepped in to shut it down. These open air makeshift tables favour Sic Bo, a dice game with quick winnings and quick turnovers.

The game is laid out on black tablecloths, ready to be bundled up before dashing in the event of a police raid.

Later, a friend tells me about the middle-class versions of these gambling dens, 'football clubs' set up with slot machines, card tables, everything except an actual football team. The police turned a blind eye, and the clubs flourished until they were eclipsed by the sleepless lights and crimson carpets of licensed Marina Bay Sands casino in 2010, where visitors can try their luck on over 500 table games. One of the games they offer is Sic Bo.

Gambling in Singapore is rolling with a weighted dice, with the odds stacked according to where you're from, where you play, and how high your stakes are. In 2020, the US Department of Justice launched an investigation into Marina Bay Sands Casino on allegations of money laundering among its top accounts.[57] Around the same time, the management hired a law firm to probe into allegations that over $1 billion of players' funds had been illicitly transferred by staff to third parties. A year before, one customer sued the casino over funds he claimed were transferred to other casino patrons without his authorization.[58] The dispute was quietly settled out of court.

'You need three main criteria to be a successful underground croupier,' Yinzhou explains. 'You need to be good with numbers. You need to be good with people. And you need to be able to run. Fast.'

9 p.m.

The courtyard is decked with fairy lights and clamour all around, with waitresses ferrying emerald bottles of Changi and honey-coloured bottles of Singha to customers crammed around tables on plastic chairs. There are steaming plates of fried noodles, bowls of thick frog leg porridge, which, of course, tastes a bit like chicken.

There are other things you can order too, off menu. This beer garden is red light lite. This is for the men who don't have the metaphorical gonads for the hourly rate at the nearby Lucky Premier Inn down the road but still fancy a quick squeeze with their Singha. This quick 'squeeze' can range anywhere from $10–$30, Yinzhou tells us, as long as it's over the T-shirt. 'Motorboating' comes at a premium of $50.

9.30 p.m.

'We're entering The Rectangle now, where the streets are divided into odd and even numbers,' Yinzhou announces. 'Married men, avoid even numbers, unless you want to make your wives very unhappy!'

Brothels! More brothels! There are 100–200 registered in Singapore, but as we snake our way down Lorong 18 and 20, it's like hopping around a Monopoly board of pleasure property. With typical diligence, Singapore has split this urban oblong by numbered streets. Numbers 15, 17, 19 for cafés, arts centres, and the General Board of True Jesus Mission. Numbers 16, 18, 20 for a different sort of sustenance, visual performance, and divine revelation.

Unlike soliciting, unlicensed gambling, and drugs, prostitution is not illegal in Singapore. Yinzhou explains that while the list of government approved source countries is unknown, most sex workers come from China, Vietnam, and Thailand. Arrivals from this shortlist come via agencies who take a hefty commission to set them up in Geylang. Money can be decent for them though, compared to back home: the average regulated Singaporean brothel worker can earn over $3,000 a month. Every three months there is a medical check, and if a woman is found to be pregnant or ill, she is immediately deported

Each house number is marked with a red light. Each woman is also given a number in the format street number–house number–person number, which makes a handy six-digit code used to pass round recommendations between regulars. These barcoded women sit outside simple massage parlours with markers or ornaments indicating their nationality to match the employees inside. Gaudy red lanterns for Chinese girls, silhouettes of thin, long-skirted dancers for Thai girls. None of them speak to us, though one or two of them smile.

10 p.m.

We're standing on a bridge, the wide Geyland Road below us, its side streets stretching out like a centipede's stubby legs. On our left hand side is a tall concrete block, one of the many dormitories where the city's migrant workers live. On the right, there is a slick new apartment complex, chirpy in its clean windows and snapshots of IKEA furniture.

Gentrification is spreading her manicured hands over this part of town, buffing its grubby edges. Over the past twenty years, Yinzhou explains, Geylang has had the highest concentration of new condominiums in Singapore. With the relocation of the Paya Lebar airbase in the 2030s will come the removal of height restrictions on new buildings and an influx of property developers rushing in to build up. What will happen then, to this carefully contained suburb of low wages and sin?

I feel like a tourist, a self-conscious voyeur. But so are the developers cashing in on Geylang's perverse trendiness, capitalizing on the fascination with the seedy, and making it palatable by sanding down its rough edges with new developments as if cleaning out a store cupboard we've been ignoring for years. It's a barrier I'll never be able to cross, a door that remains closed. Who knows the real Geylang apart from the people who call it home?

10.30 p.m.

We are in front of an unremarkable apartment block in a quiet side street. It's an anticlimactic end to our sightseeing tour of sin. A slightly open window exhales a curl of steam on the ground floor. A pair of checked boxers and a red T-shirt with a nineties movie logo stretch across a thin washing line outside.

Yinzhou has lived in the same house for every one of his twenty-seven years. Growing up in these rooms, he'd play badminton on the community courts with a group of young migrant workers from Bangladesh. This is the thing about these areas that are ostracized and fetishized as the 'rough areas of town'. They can break down barriers that might exist elsewhere, divisions of race, gender, sexuality, blurred by the commonality of living together on the outside.

One day, while playing badminton in the back alley, they were met with routine ground surveillance. Upon seeing his identity card, the officers were puzzled that he, as a Singaporean, was hanging out with 'them', the migrant workers.

'But, why?' they asked, bewildered. 'Why are you friends with these people?'

Sometimes, he still wonders what happened to them. There are questions in Geylang that even its long-time residents, those who've spent their lives among the numerically divided streets and dedicated their careers towards its tours of sin, don't have the answers to.

Helen

I meet Helen over a bag of condoms. It is evening in Geylang. The sky is smudgy grey, except around the bungalows where dim street lights and hanging lanterns bleed yellow and red into the outside air.

I am with a non-profit organization called Project X. They hand out condoms like canapes at a conference. Helen knows everyone by name, making friendly small talk as she fishes a condom out of their bag. She is red-haired and casually dressed—bright yellow silk top over dark jeans. She is a few months away from her fifty-eighth birthday, and her fingers are topped by ten smooth glossy ovals of polish.

There are two types of sex workers in Geylang. There are those who work at regulated brothels and are themselves registered and subject to government regulations and restrictions. Then there are the freelancers: the renegades, the women who want to do things on their own terms. Helen belongs to the second category. We sit down in an open-air café, the table and chairs bright blocks of bottle green. 'I set my own rates. I choose my own clients,' she says, tapping her perfectly manicured fingers on the shared acrylic table. 'If they want something weird, then I charge a little bit extra.'

Helen grew up in Queenstown, a formerly swampy southwestern suburb, which has now been taken over by demure low-rise residential blocks. Helen was not always Helen, just as Helen was not always a sex worker. Once, she was the eldest son of a Chinese family, a young boy with crushes on her male classmates, who knew early on that she was transgender but kept it from her parents until after National Service 'because I knew it would be terrible'. 'They didn't agree at first,' she says. 'They wanted me to have a normal life and a traditional family. I tried to change myself but I couldn't do anything about it.'

Singapore was the first country in Asia to legalize gender-affirming surgery in 1973. Once they have undergone surgery, transgender Singaporeans are able to officially change their gender on their identity cards. They are able to get married, as long as it's a heteronormative partnership. Transgender women who have fully transitioned and have legal status are exempt from National Service. But until then, they're in limbo, as, Helen says, they're 'not real women'.

She tried other jobs too, 'normal jobs that would have made my parents happy'. She worked in sales, customer service, retail boutiques. 'But I could never really adapt. I was really sensitive. After taking hormones you get really sensitive! And people would call me "Ladyboy" and pinpoint me.' Sex work to her seemed, ironically, to be a role without judgement, a job outside the structures of 'normal' society, where you could be both someone else entirely and completely yourself. 'Plus,' Helen adds, 'the money was really good in the eighties.'

They would start at Newton, a bustling circus of 'great food and tourists who knew they could come [here] for a good time.' Then, they would shift to Orchard Road around 1 a.m. and skirt their way around the bars and nightclubs, sometimes ending up at a nondescript oblong building with an underground reputation, if work was flagging and the bars were closed. 'People always think we spend all night at Orchard Towers,' she says. 'But Orchard Towers isn't where you start. Orchard Towers is where you end up if business is bad.'

She moved to Geylang in 2019, the same year thirty-one-year-old Singaporean Satheesh Noel Gobidass was stabbed to death in a fight at Orchard Towers. His hat was retrieved from one of his favourite bars.

In 2022, the government announced that all entertainment venues in Orchard Towers would not have their licences renewed past May 2023. Business bled out into other areas of Singapore, and Helen followed.

Helen's day starts at 3 p.m. 'I normally sleep late. I don't sleep that well. It's the drugs and the hormones that keep me up.' She takes a couple of hours to get ready, then arrives at Geylang as the evening hits; and the men—office workers, construction workers, and conference delegates still wearing their lanyards—shuffle coyly past closed doors.

In the budget hotel rooms rented by the hour, clients tell Helen their deepest secrets and private kinks. 'Sometimes it's anal. Sometimes, they want to pee on me. Sometimes they just want to be tied up for an hour. That's their fantasy, I can't say anything. I'm just there to make them feel good.'

Once, a man came in and stripped down to reveal a G-string and a bra covering a pert pair of breasts.

Sometimes they're violent. She's heard one or two stories of girls left lifeless on hotel beds. It's hard to go to the police when your job is in the grey areas of the law.[59] Eventually, the girls' deaths were put down to an overdose.

'Once a guy tried to squeeze me around the neck,' she recalls. 'Luckily I was big enough to hold him off.'

The government, she believes, is doing everything it can. They turn a blind eye to most of the illegal solicitation gatherings on the sidelines of Geylang's brothels, she says. That's the price of relative autonomy. When you're operating on the edges of the law, calling the police becomes a double-edged sword. Helen and other freelance sex workers rely on advocacy groups like Project X for monthly health checks and condoms.

The regulated brothels provide competition. There are fewer people now and more girls. Younger girls, 'exotic' girls from Thailand or Vietnam, playing up the fetishization of their cultures.

'Geylang's changed now,' says Helen, with the nostalgia of a sector veteran remembering an industry boom. 'I used to have four, five clients a night. Now, I am lucky if I have one.'

Helen has changed too. 'I'm more mature now,' she says, 'with thicker skin. I say to myself, "You're a sex worker. Go for it!"' Her relationship with her family has come full circle, and she's recently moved back into the family home, not as her parents' first son but as their eldest daughter.

'I have a good relationship with my parents,' she says. 'I send them money, and I help support them. But Chinese families are always a bit funny about [sex work]. When they see me go out, they will ask, "Hey! Why you wearing so short?" All parents are the same.'

The tables are clearing around us. Half-finished plates of fried Maggi noodles and half-drained cups of fiery calamansi juice are fed to gaping bins. The night is ending. The night is just starting. Helen is thinking forward.

'Right now, my hope for the future is just to be happy and to have money coming in,' she says. 'I'm getting older. Before, I wanted to go overseas and work. My friends who worked there would show me pictures of London, of Europe. The escorts there!'

The car headlights beam a dim glow across the streets. This is Helen. Sex worker. Member of the trans community. And a woman with big dreams, smaller dreams, and the best nails I've ever seen.

Disneyland with the Death Penalty

Protesting has procedure in Singapore.

Public demonstrations are allowed if you apply for a police permit and comply with a designated set of guidelines set under the Public Order Act. Gatherings without a permit must be apolitical; they must be non-aggressive; they must not stir up uneasy memories by commemorating a significant event.[60] Protesting with a permit is polite and Singaporean. Protesting with a permit is not a protest but a process.

The one place Singaporeans can protest without a permit is Hong Lim Park at its Speakers' Corner. Singapore's first public garden was built in the nineteenth century and has storytelling in its roots. During its time, the lawn held an open-air theatre and public movie screenings and, in the early years of independence, hosted several political rallies.

For one warm night in 2022, the grass glowed with a crowd of wobbly candle flames and signs that read 'Abolish the death penalty!' and 'Don't kill in our name!'

Around four hundred people gathered that day in protest against the execution of inmates on Changi Prison's death row. One inmate was Nagaenthran K. Dharmalingam, a thirty-three-year-old Malaysian man with alleged intellectual disabilities. He had been in prison for over ten years since he was caught smuggling 43 grams of heroin strapped to his left thigh as he crossed from Malaysia to Singapore. He was hanged that week.[61]

Singapore is one of the fifty-five countries in the world that still maintain the death penalty. An article from 2023 stated that the city-state hanged sixteen people since resuming state executions in March 2022. All of those executed were low- to mid-level drug offenders convicted for trafficking drugs.[62] Anyone caught trafficking more than 500 grams of cannabis or 250 grams of methamphetamine can be sentenced to death under the Misuse of Drugs Act. Disneyland with the Death Penalty, I've heard it called. An adult playground with a sinister side.

I've learned from my Geylang adventures that there is an element of looking away when it comes to drug activity. But society needs examples. It needs cautionary case studies to deter the underground trend from entering the mainstream and to maintain the city-state's hard-earned image of safety and social order.

One year and several executions later, news broke about Tangaraju Suppiah.

Tangaraju, a forty-six-year old Tamil Singaporean mini-mart owner had been apprehended by the police in 2014 for drug consumption and failure to report for a drug test. While detained, officers investigated him for suspected links to two men who'd been arrested over a delivery of cannabis the year before. According to campaigners, Tangaraju was only partially tied to the offence.[63]

During his police questioning, family members and activists say, Tangaraju asked for a Tamil interpreter as he didn't understand the English statement being read out to him. He was refused.[64] Later, when his family tried to find a lawyer to represent him, no one was willing to take on the case, fearing personal cost or censure from the court. With no legal training, Tangaraju decided to represent himself.[65] The Singapore government has denied all these claims.[66]

'Access to justice is a real problem in Singapore. There is no access to legal counsel during interrogation by the police,[67] and the statements don't have to be taken verbatim,' comments Kirsten Han, a Singaporean journalist and anti-death penalty activist. 'So it really comes down to how able the individual is in advocating for themselves and being aware of the potential implications of such statements being used against them in court.'

Tangaraju lost his case and a later appeal. He was executed on 26 April 2023.

His hanging took place against the background of a slow shift in Southeast Asia. The month Tangaraju died, Malaysia voted to abolish the mandatory death penalty for twelve sentences, including drug trafficking. The summer before, Thailand had made moves to decriminalize marijuana, spiking a surge in pop-up cannabis cafés. But still, Singapore remained steadfast. The findings of a survey in 2023 showed that around 77 per cent of Singaporean respondents strongly agreed or agreed that the death penalty should be used for the most serious crimes.[68]

The government needs examples, faces to put behind the statistics, and many of these are brown faces, with Tamil and Malaysian names.[69]

'A lot of the people who get arrested for capital charges . . . tend to be people from very vulnerable backgrounds,' remarked Singaporean human rights activist and researcher Kokila Annamalai after Tangaraju's execution. 'They overwhelmingly tend to be ethnic minorities and non-native English speakers with lower education levels.'

I am a foreigner and we're not allowed to protest, not even in Hong Lim Park. It's not our country and not our business. Speaking out about another country's social issues is a bit like commenting on another family's dirty laundry. Plus, Singapore has been good to us. Rocking the boat might cost us our visa. So we stay quiet, keep our heads down, and wait for the storm to pass.

But still, we can hear the last hopes of desperate families. We can listen to the groups swimming against the tide of social order. And we can see hundreds of tiny lights in Hong Lim Park. Waving. Flickering. Waiting for change.

DOWN TO EARTH

Collecting Memories

Alvin Yapp has over 300 women's shoes. Each one is lined up neatly next to its partner. They fill display cabinets in the mezzanine of his house, their pointed toes slanting downwards, their beaded bodies catching the light.

Alvin is an antiques collector and curator of the Intan, a private museum dedicated to Peranakan artifacts. The slippers share the top floor with soft silk kebaya shirts and a curtained four-poster bed, its red silk hangings embroidered with gold phoenixes. Bulbous enameled spittoons stand to attention on the wooden stairs. On the ground floor, Alvin serves guests seated in dark lacquered thrones inlaid with surly grey mother-of-pearl traditional kueh cake and tea from a repoussé silver teapot. The whole place is a wonderland, a crowded, perfectly curated jumble of history, memories, and bold, glittering colour. It is Alvin's home.

'I never meant it to be a museum,' he tells me. 'I started to collect antiques as a kid. That was my way of learning about my own culture.'

Peranakan heritage lies in the networks of settlers—from China and elsewhere—who arrived in the Malacca Straits during the fifteenth century and adopted the culture, often by marrying into local families. Peranakan is derived from the Malay for 'local born', and according to legend, the term was first used when a Chinese princess was wed into the Malay sultanate, and her male entourage made their own bonds with the indigenous women. Their children were the first Peranakans.

Chinese Peranakan clothes weave together different strands of heritage. The *nyonya kebaya* is an outfit derived from the Malay long dress *baju panjang* and the keyaba jacket is said to have drawn inspiration from the *qaba*, a robe popular among the nobility of the middle east, central Asia, and North India since the ninth century. The bright beaded slippers draw from Chinese, Malay, and European designs.

Along with the self-proclaimed 'babas' and 'nyonyas', mainly descended from Hokkien speaking Chinese, there are Jawi Peranakans of mixed Indian and Malay Muslim heritage, Arab Perankans, Java Peranakans. Peranakan culture is a cornerstone of split identity, which was what started Alvin on his heritage collecting journey in the first place.

'When I was in school, everyone expected me to speak Mandarin because I looked Chinese, even though at home we spoke English. When I went to my grandma's house, the food, the songs, everything was different [from my Chinese classmates]. I was a young kid, and I was trying to discover my own identity, [but] I didn't know who I was. And I carried a lot of confusion because of that.'

What do you do when you're an invisible minority, when your features or the colour of your skin slot you into a majority where you don't quite fit? What do you do when your heritage lies not in appearances but in objects (the brightly glazed ceramics overlaid with phoenixes, peonies, or other auspicious motifs) and dishes (*babi pongteh* pork in fermented soy beans, *ayam buah keluak* chicken stew with heavy black *keluak* nuts bobbing in sharp tamarind gravy)?

This is the way my dad remembers his grandmother—through shreds of colour and taste and sound and stories. The glint of the gold buttons on her neatly pressed kebaya. Chalky white *kueh bangkit*, tapioca biscuits in the shape of animals, crispy triangle 'love letter' biscuits. The scraping sound of the pestle and mortar as she pounded dark red chillies into sambal belacan paste.

Chinese Peranakans believed in the united power of a mortar and grinder—separating them meant disunity and bad luck. Sometimes, matchmakers or mothers-in-law would listen to the sound of a prospective daughter-in-law grinding chillies to judge her suitability to join the family.

I'd never heard the word Peranakan before I moved to Singapore. I wasn't one of those Brits who asked earnestly if Singapore was part of China. But still, to me, Singaporeans were Singaporeans. I was blithely ignorant of the different ethnic groups, proudly preserving their heritage and sharing their culture, even the one I happened to be a part of.

Alvin started haunting antique dealers and estate sales, bidding on snapshots of his Peranakan heritage. 'At first, I was mainly collecting things people didn't want, because my finances weren't great,' he remembers. 'And I collected some wrong things.' But his knowledge grew with his collection, and eventually, he found people asking to visit his home, to learn more about Peranakan culture. Some, like him, had grown up in Peranakan households; they recognized the colours and shapes of their family history without knowing the stories behind them.

In 2010, Alvin was approached by the National Heritage Board and his private collection became a museum. It now welcomes up to 200 visitors a month and has won a number of heritage awards. But for him, the most important part is meeting different guests every week, sharing 'insight[s] into the lifestyle and personality of the Peranakan community' over hot tea and kueh cake.

Celebrating your heritage is, Alvin points out, a luxury. When he was growing up in the sixties, people were more preoccupied with looking forward than looking back. 'Museums were less important to nation building, finding jobs or people building houses or getting the economy running as a young and not so wealthy country,' he explains. 'We never needed to ask ourselves "Who is a Singaporean?" "What is a Singaporean?" until much later.' It was hard to learn much about Peranakan heritage, so much of their history was told orally, passed down like family recipes from generation to generation.

Now, Peranakan culture has taken on a sort of trendiness. Alvin notes a growing interest, especially among mainland Chinese visitors who are tracking the fates of their itinerant ancestors. Alvin's Intan isn't the only place celebrating the community. The white-columned galleries of the Peranakan Museum chart the home, life, and cuisine of Southeast Asia's Peranakan communities. Galleries in Chinatown sell rows of cheerful ceramic tiles affluent Peranakan families bought off nineteenth century European and twentieth century Japanese manufacturers and incorporated as distinctive features of their own interior design. Restaurants serve *babi pongteh* and *nyonya laksa*. Accounts on TikTok and Instagram celebrate the customs, cakes, and clothes of 'being Peranakan'.

Alvin tells me about a video he saw on social media recently of a bride choosing an embroidered nyonya kebaya for her wedding. It was in blue and white, traditional colours of mourning, but for him, as long as the wearer knows the original meaning of the garment, it's up to her to give tradition new context. Heritage and history are consistently evolving, changing, and adapting. It's what the original Peranakan settlers with their hybrid customs and their mixed-race marriages did themselves.

And in the midst of this is a constant collector, the same boy on a private search for himself, even as his museum and culture become more visible, celebrated, and recognized. Marking his heritage through antique furniture, brightly-coloured cakes, and hundreds of decorative shoes. A journey of self-discovery on public display, but where the most important things are still kept private.

Alvin's favourite item in his collection is a simple pair of low-heeled beaded slippers, 'The last thing I have from my grandmother,' he says. They are not on display.

Haw Par Villa

It is hot in Hell. It's hot everywhere in Singapore these days. The June air is smudgy and dense with the transboundary haze that spreads from the burning forests in Indonesia. It adds to the apocalyptic vibe but not as much as the figure being dismembered in front of me.

Haw Par Villa is the largest outdoor sculpture park in the country. The villa was built by Myanmar-born entrepreneur Aw Boon Haw in memory of his younger brother and business partner Aw Boon Par in 1937. It is the creepiest manifestation of brotherly love I have ever seen.

Boon Haw was a keen philanthropist and advocate of the ethics of Chinese Confucianism, and the place is like a Tim Burton-esque theme park of Chinese folklore. The Eight Immortals trek across a powder-blue plaster sea. The Three Sisters throw magical scissors to behead their enemies in the Battle of the Yellow River. There is a painted lake, with life-size statues of bare-breasted mermaids, for reasons not quite explained.

A panoply of vices and virtues, like puppet shows on pause, show miniature representations of the real-life opium trading and gambling that was dirtying the city-state's pristine social fabric during the thirties. One scene shows a model jazz club, a pretty singer sensually caressing a microphone. It is meant to warn against wasting wealth on the vices of wine and women.

And there is Hell. This version has ten caverns. Each one is manned by a judge who decides your fate according to a very specific set of crimes and punishments. Lack of filial piety gets your intestines removed. Spread rumours and you find your tongue wrenched from your mouth. The plaster man in front of me in the process of being sawn bloodily in half was apparently someone who possessed pornography, wasted food, or misused books. It isn't mentioned what metrics were used to match misdeeds to forfeits but judging from the man being shredded to death on a tree of knives, they really didn't like curse words.

'Enjoy your visit!' says the cheery collar-shirted student manning the ticket desk.

The Aw brothers built an empire off Tiger Balm. If you've never tried Tiger Balm before, imagine a menthol glacier freezing your nerves, from the inside, then overpowering you with heat. There are camphor and cloves in there too. It's a sticky, waxy magic potion that will kill your headache or chest infection while leaving your nasal cavities as scorched as an Indonesian forest fire during haze season. It's the go-to over-the-counter cure in many Asian families, which is how the Aw family made their fortune.

By a montage of a man being heavily crushed under a stone mallet (tax evasion), a small girl is hiding her face and crying. Her mother is nagging her, urging her to open her eyes, to be brave and see the underworld for all its gore, guts, and gory. *I feel you, kid*, I think. *I've been you before.*

I last went to Haw Par Villa with Mum when I was six years old. She'd come back to Singapore because Dad had taken on a short-term post with an American bank looking to expand their presence in Asia. She'd also come back to chase ghosts. Her father had died and there was a cavern in her stomach, a hunger to find her roots.

But Singapore had changed. There was a new prime minister, Goh Chok Tong, who touted 'The Next Lap' of Singapore. There was a new terminal at Changi airport to build on the existing 1,900 weekly flights to 111 cities in fifty-two countries.[70] There was Asia's largest tropical oceanarium, a $20 million monster with a winding acrylic tunnel where you could watch fish from the deep.

In the years after they married, they built a series of short lives lived out in two-year intervals across various international cities. Mum was a project manager in Boston, turning heads on the trading floor in stilettos and shoulder pads. The family breadwinner in the boys' club of eighties finance, while Dad studied for his MBA. She was a secretary at the British embassy in Tokyo, heavily pregnant and able to slip back for lunchtime naps in their flat in Chiyoda. She developed an obsession with finding a 'forever home', a pressure that got bigger with every move, which set the standards of this ideal house so high that no estate agent could find it.

Fear fuels us. The garish painted monsters that tell us that we're not doing the right thing, that we should keep our head down and our feet on the straight and narrow—haunting us with phantoms of what might happen if we don't. Fear can keep us running from country to country or make us seek home before we're ready.

She renounced her Singaporean passport years before. Singapore doesn't allow dual citizenship. You are in or out, fully committed to the Singapore story or not at all. Like a romantic partnership, loyalty to your country and no other. If I'd been born a boy, or Lil Sis had been Lil Bro, we would have had to serve two years of National Service as soon as we turned eighteen, whether or not we'd ever set foot on the Little Red Dot.

Singapore is a country of travellers. It's bred a culture of dynamism and courage in its people. Plus, it's a small island, so even Singaporeans get itchy feet and want to explore. They move abroad for work, for education, for love. Those that eventually decide to trade in their passport for the same reason have described receiving a long, detailed questionnaire, asking them in probing detail why they want to leave.

'Like a rejected lover who wants to know why you're breaking up with them,' says a family friend who went through the process. Another recalls going to the High Commission in London, where they asked her if she was really sure she wanted to do this, before cutting up her passport in front of her. Singapore is proud of its Singaporeans. It wants to keep them.

My mum received an official letter stamped with the Singaporean coat of arms and was requested to send back her ID card. She can't remember if they interrogated her or cut up her passport, but there was an aftertaste of loss, an inkling that she was giving up a small part of herself.

There's a Singlish word *kiasu*, which means fear of losing or missing out. There's another, *kiasi*, which sounds almost exactly the same and means fear of death. Is there a word for fear of not settling, of always feeling rootless, misplaced?

'Enjoy the rest of your afternoon,' trills the attendant as I exit Hell via the gift shop. That's the nice thing about Haw Par Villa, we can leave the afterworld behind. The real demons are those that we carry with us, a bit like the skull-imprinted Haw Par Villa tote bags, keeping us always searching, always running, always looking for more.

The Last Kampung

'Lorong Buangkok,' says my taxi driver, looking at the GPS. He says it with a flourish, as if he's talking about a rare sighting of an almost extinct species. 'The last of the kampungs.'

Once, Singapore was full of kampungs. These small traditional villages were the main hubs of community living before the high-rises took over the skyline in the mass urbanization movements of the eighties. Now, they surf the wavelengths of nostalgia in the phrase 'kampung spirit', describing the essence of community that connected these brick-and-wood slat bungalows, or in the memories of older generations reminiscing as the hum of a hyperconnected modern world pulses in the present.

Kampungs are a dream, a leafy vestige that remind us of what we were before progress and its ultimate crushing power, because all the kampungs are gone now. Except Lorong Buangkok.

'Just be prepared, people may give you strange looks,' the taxi driver says as he drops me at the top of a dusty side street. 'These residents know each other. To them, you are like alien.'

One of Lorong Buangkok's long-term residents is the driving force behind its survival. The land is privately owned by Sng Mui Hong, who grew up in the village and is the daughter of a Chinese medicine seller who owned the freehold to the kampung. Since she inherited the estate, Sng has received numerous offers to buy the land; valued at reportedly up to $70 million. But she's refused every one and continues to charge residents a token monthly rent ranging from around $4 to $30.

Now in her seventies, I've read Sng's interviews where she speaks to journalists at the site of her former home, which has become a film set. She welcomes excursions where locals invite urban children to play traditional pre-technology games. That's the price of preservation: packaging heritage to appeal to public nostalgia. I want to see what Lorong Buangkok looks like outside the eyes of the tour groups.

It is quiet. The streets are empty apart from a couple of stray cats sheltering under the shade of parked cars. Zinc sheet roofs reflect the harsh sunlight off baby blue and pastel pink bungalows. An exercise bike stands on one wooden porch, a flourish of plastic sunflowers winds its stems round the rails of another. Through the walls I can hear the slow mumble of a television show and a family bickering. The whole area is cocooned, sheltered from the rest of the world by borders of thick green. The only signs of reality are the occasional parked Mercedes in a bungalow driveway and the tips of apartment blocks peering above the trees' peaks.

I dodge a few chickens scratching dust off a path that leads to a deep red house with an open door. A Malay man with a neat goatee is standing in its frame and, as predicted, staring at me like I'm an alien as I stammer an introduction.

'Are you from London?' he asks eventually. 'I recognize the accent. I studied at Loughborough.'

Nassib has lived in the kampung since he married his wife Lina twenty-eight years ago. While he prepares for Friday prayers, I help Lina shift palm fronds the size of her torso. The house was her father's. Only relatives of Lorong Buangkok's original residents are allowed to rent here, she says.

It seemed bigger then, she remembers. 'Now, we have public housing in front of us. And private housing behind us. We're boxed in. But our life isn't so different [to theirs]. We're very ordinary.'

Lina's father worked for the Institute of Mental Health (IMH). The psychiatric hospital used to be in one of the nearby tower blocks, and many of the Lorong Buangkok parents were also IMH staff. The families were tight-knit, and the children played together. 'Now,' Lina says, 'we know our neighbours, but people stay inside their houses. Keep to themselves.'

But the kampung is still 'less peaceful' than she remembers. 'Because now everybody knows about this place. It's on YouTube. There are tourists. Just this morning a group of students came on bikes from a school in Sengkang.'

She doesn't mind the visitors. Her siblings have moved to the city centre, and her nieces and nephews have been raised on a diet of screens, social media, and concrete sidewalks. 'It's important to teach them about what it's like here, what it was like before,' she says. 'Because we don't know if this place will be here forever.'

While Sng holds the freehold indefinitely, the government maintains the right to acquire it at any time.

Because no matter how romanticism might paint it, Lorong Buangkok is not in a time capsule, and nor is Lina. Rows of freshly-washed clothes sway from the washing line, a medley of traditional Malay dresses and T-shirts from high-end brands. As she's sharing encyclopaedic knowledge of which bus routes will take me back to the city centre, a scuttle of movement shoots up the left side of her head. 'There's a lizard on your sun hat,' I point out. She shrugs. 'Leave it,' she says. 'It'll move on eventually. Everything always does.'

We try to bottle nostalgia. We pocket idealized snapshots of the past as the 'good old days'. We share stories about the bulldozers that razed family homes and split communities or the memory of the floods across the low-lying plane. *Selak kain*—the hitching of sarong hems to stop them getting soaked—is Lorong Buangkok's Malay nickname. We try to recreate the best parts of our past in our present, moving forward while also looking back. We want it all.

The government has apparently made a conscious effort to recreate the kampung spirit through a focus on communal spaces in HDB apartments.

A few weeks later, I am in an open air *kopitiam* in Duxton, behind the turquoise gates of the Sri Layan Sithi Vinayagar Temple. The colourful shophouses nearby frosted with ornate plaster trimmings used to be fronts for a thriving red-light district. I'm sipping tea cloudy with condensed milk with business trainer and professional singer, K. Kamalanathan. He grew up in a kampung during the sixties, during Singapore's transition to independence. For him and his neighbours, kampung spirit was a way of coming together as a small, fledgling country, a feeling 'of unity, of togetherness, [the feeling] that we didn't need anyone else'.

'It was a huge Chinese kampung,' he tells me. 'But right at the end, there was a big Malay enclave, and we had a few Indian families in the area.' Nearby was one of the biggest Chinese temples in the neighbourhood, and Kamalanathan remembers all the families coming together every night for the month-long Hungry Ghost festivities.

'My school was just three minutes away from our house,' he remembers. 'In the evening, I could just run out and play with my brothers in the school field, come back all drenched in mud. Of course, we'd get a good beating from my father. But there was a lot of fun [at that time].'

The kampung was razed in the mid-seventies to make way for industrial and housing estates.

In his current HDB high-rise, people are polite. Neighbours acknowledge each other. When I ask about the presence of 'kampung spirit', he recounts the time he found himself in a lift with a Chinese mother and her young son.

'The boy pointed at me and said, "*Apu nehneh! Apu nehneh!*" he recalls with a small smile. 'I think he was maybe about seven or eight years old.' The phrase, originally derived from a casual Indian greeting, has become adopted by others as a racial slur, gathering problematic undertones with time, like moss on a stone.

We can't recreate the past, not really. There is too much baggage, too much movement, too much 'now' leaving fingerprints on our memories. Besides, memories are messy and murky. We like to remember the good old days, forget the bad and painful until the next time, until something happens that reminds us how much a simple phrase has changed, or just how far we've come.

'Families have become more affluent now. Singapore has become richer,' says Kamalanathan. 'People do much better in life. I guess there's always a trade-off.'

All we can do is look forward and try to make sure that the forward we're looking towards is one we're proud of. Teach our children not just about what sort of past we had but also what sort of future they want. And when we change, do everything we can to make sure it's not for the worse.

The second last kampung on Singapore's mainland was demolished in 2007.[71] Some of the former village areas have been turned into military training grounds. Some areas have been earmarked for conservation, snake-like mangrove roots dipping into untamed watery plains. In the meantime, Lorong Buangkok, the last kampung, carries on in peaceful limbo, changing even as it steadfastly stays the same. It will move on eventually. Everything always does.

Otters

There's a misconception that Singapore is lacking in green spaces. They're there, folded into the city's meticulous urban planning, offshoot legacies of Lee Kuan Yew's 1967 vision of building a 'garden city'. Climate urgency has ramped up the heat—the national Green Plan 2030 promises that 50 per cent more land will be dedicated to nature parks, from a 2020 baseline, and that everyone will live within a ten-minute walk from a park before the end of the decade.

Until then, there are pockets: the mirror smooth surfaces of MacRitchie Reservoir, the grassy wetlands of Sungei Buloh, Kranji marshes, where an eccentric and wonderful millionaire and her husband run an urban farm stretching across fields of local fruit, vegetables, and herbs.

There is also Punggol. Punggol, where the water stretches a dull jade green under wide bridges, where migrant workers sleep in the shade on their breaks. There are boardwalks that look out onto glassy reservoirs. And there are otters.

Otters are a favourite local animal in Singapore. They hold an advantage over the Merlion by virtue of not being fictional. They are also very cute. Their wide-faced furry appeal is so indisputable that it has already been used for political purposes, the Progress Singapore Party adopted a series of button-nosed otter plushies as their mascot. There are two types of otters in Singapore: the Asian small-clawed otters and smooth-coated otters. And while destruction of habitat and water pollution led to this aquatic teddy-bear nearing extinction in Singapore in the sixties, recently populations have been thriving. The small-clawed and the smooth-coated have inter-married and Singapore now boasts around 170 otters, and numerous mixed-race otter families.[72]

You can call a group of otters a bevy, a raft, a lodge, or a romp, depending on your mood and whether they're in the water or not.

Catching a glimpse of otters becomes a temporary fix, the way everyone temporarily became hooked on catching Pokémon in 2016. I see a group gambolling down the bank and take a short video of them. My video is two-seconds long and like something out of *The Blair Witch Project*. There's the sound of semi-aquatic mammalian shrieking and a flash of a tail before the shy celebrities hurry off the edge of the screen. This, in my defence, is because otters are pretty fast. They run up to speeds of 15 miles per hour, and they can slide even faster. Those at Punggol clump together in a sleek bevy, rolling around in the dust by the riverbanks, then sliding like long, furry arrows into the water.

Otters hold hands in the water, to keep from floating away from each other while they sleep. They also sometimes violently rape otter corpses and hold otter pups hostage for food, but as that's less cute, it is less propagated as a bit of animal trivia. They are playful and social, pack-based animals, like dogs, or humans. Once, we saw an otter family in the Botanic Gardens screaming hysterically at one pup who was hesitating to jump in the brook and join the rest of the clan on the other side. The noise was like a school sports day, but with the opposite message. No one gets left behind.

Billboards deck the paths promising a bright future for Punggol. As the water-town soaks up gentrification, skeletons of new buildings and foetuses of condominiums to come cast their reflections over the river. 'These illustrations are just the artist's interpretation,' warn the signs, in case their grinning multiracial families and blueprints of smart city hubs and apartments with organic cafés in the lobbies are promising dreams they may not be able to realize, dreams they can't be held accountable for.

I don't know what will happen to the resident Punggol otters as these ambitious plans take root. Maybe they're hardened urbanites now, not to be thrown by a generation of Singaporean yuppies. Maybe they'll be on the move again, a tight clump, a furry raft, floating through the ravines in search of their next home.

Pulau Ubin

Singapore is not an island. This is one of the most common myths about it. In fact, the country is made up of around sixty-four islands, including the main one where most people live. There is Sentosa, home to theme parks, casinos, and carefully-manicured private coves housing elusive businessmen and their bullet-sleek yachts. To the South, Lazarus and St. John's, where what used to be a housing base for political detainees and secret society ringleaders is now full of popular weekend spots, with milky beaches garnished with picnic mats and swimmers leaving footprints towards the waves. Kusu, named after the legendary tortoise that turned itself into an island to save two shipwrecked sailors, hosts a crimson-pillared temple and a tiny sanctuary for the shelled reptiles.

Off the northeastern coast of Singapore is an island frozen in time. Pulau Ubin is a boomerang-shaped island, around 8 kilometres long, where around thirty-eight residents live a life unrecognizable from the busy commercial metropolis of the mainland's city centre. Only a few cars drive down the dusty main road, where stray dogs sunbathe and open-air eating houses sell plates of local kampung chicken and small mugs of steaming sweet *kopi*.

You reach Pulau Ubin by bumboat. There is a haphazard queuing system, and flip-flop clad boatmen usher you in groups of twelve from Changi Ferry Point terminal across wooden decks and onto slat board benches that sit behind the bow. The city's skyline glints and shrinks, and your legs are splattered with salty spray as you screech away from the mainland. There's a bronze statue of a hand on Changi beach, its index finger pointing upwards, towards God or God knows what.

The island's name is Malay for 'Granite Island', and Pulau Ubin was known originally for the quarries where the rock is mined. There were up to 4,000 people living on the island in the seventies. Most were Chinese, the next largest ethnic group was Malay, a few were Indian. But on a landmass that small, there was no room for Raffles' ethnic delineations. They worked together in the quarries, in the coffee plantations, as fishermen, or farmed for prawns in the bunds that fused a cluster of what had once been five smaller islands into one. They trickled out with the gradual closing of quarries, until the last one shut down in 1999.

Now, you can rent bikes for around $10 a day. They're no steel stallions but having your gear chain slip and your leg stabbed by your kick brake while furiously peddling through grasslands starts to feel a bit like part of the time capsule experience, like the wood board houses with their wide windows, corrugated iron roofs, and bright paint. There are snapshots of local life, both past and present. A carcass of a former local provision shop, preserved as a baby-blue and butter-yellow wooden example of rustic architecture, sits down the road from a porch populated with Chinese calligraphy paintings and a man speaking urgent Cantonese into a radio.

We cycle past the olive-green water of the Jalan Ubin lotus pond and the hushed shade of the Muslim cemetery. We grab huge gulps of air that smells of *pandan*. Paul's pace is constant, steady, I work in stops and starts, rushing eagerly ahead, then cruising, before accelerating again. There's probably some metaphorical life insight here, but I'm too focused on whether my bike will fall apart to figure it out.

There is a shrine dedicated to a German girl who fell off a cliff while fleeing from the British in 1914. There is a temple dedicated to Ma Zu, the goddess who would bring safety to sailors and fishermen.

There were rubber plantations here once, among the coconut trees, by the boardwalk and the dense soil that now forms wetlands. Many of the country's smooth trunks pumping milky sap like new mothers were overtaken during the Japanese occupation, and after the war, cheaper labour brought the rubber boom to Malaysia.

On the closest thing Pulau Ubin has to a high street, a curving dusty street flanked by bicycle shops and cafés advertising fresh cold serves of ice *kacang*, *cendol*, and young coconut, we find Mr Tan. He sells us cool metal cans of iced coffee from the fridge in his café stall, a business he inherited from his father. Mr Tan was born on the island and still lives here but also has a home on the mainland, an umbilical cord tying him to modernity.

'My day off is every Tuesday,' he tells us, jabbing a finger at the date on the Chinese newspaper in front of him. 'I go to the main island. I go shopping. I buy things. I buy vegetables. Then I bring them back. It is hard work, and a lot of pressure but I would never leave the island. I was born here. It's my home.'

'Things change on the island,' Mr. Tan says, 'but they change slowly, slowly. So slowly, you barely realize it.' The bulky bright freezer box selling supermarket brand ice-creams. Sweaty tourists with American and British accents, driving dust tracks through his high street or bombarding him eagerly with semi-intrusive questions about his personal life. In 2005, Mr Tan's family bought the restaurant next to his café, a spacious open-air seafood food court, filled with activewear and the smell of crayfish, steamed and fried in fresh garlic. It's busy, I remark to Mr Tan, but he shakes his head. 'Before, there were over three times, four times as many people on the island,' he says firmly.

About 300,000 people come to Pulau Ubin a year, according to the National Parks Board. But they are transient visitors. During some weekdays, the island is a ghost town. The residents of the island will slowly drift towards the mainland. Things change, slowly, slowly, but inevitably. You can't stay frozen in time forever.

Legend has it that one day, three animals decided to have a race. An elephant, a frog, and a pig; each thought that they were the fastest swimmer and set the watery distance that separated Singapore's coast from the Malaysian state of Johor as a way to find out. Anyone who failed to complete the race would be turned into stone.

They launched themselves confidently into the waves and all was going well, until a strong current arrived. The animals started to struggle—two of them were land creatures after all—and, eventually, the swell pulled them underwater. The frog became Pulau Sekudu, wedged between Serangoon Harbour and the Chek Jawa Wetlands. The pig and the elephant became Pulau Ubin, all three of them rooted together forever in the grip of the ultimate winner: the ocean.

Riot Island

On a sluggish, humid day on 12 July 1963, Mohammad Bin Poh overslept.

The nineteen-year-old boatman was three weeks into his new job as part of a pioneering new prison project on Pulau Senang, an 81.7 hectare coral island about 13 kilometres off Singapore's southern coast. Bin Poh had meant to get up in the morning. Instead, he was rattled awake in the heat of an early afternoon by explosions. He rose to the sight of burning buildings and about thirty detainees running towards his sleeping quarters.

He raced to his boat, alerting police through the portable radio used to maintain communication with the mainland. When he returned to the main campus, the first thing he saw was the bodies of his colleagues—hacked brutally by knives, tools, and broken bottles.

'Some of them were hit by the prisoners, some were smashed [up], some were cut, like people cutting fish,' Bin Poh recalls sixty years later from the sofa of his HDB flat. 'Three [of my coworkers] died on the island. Another died later in hospital.'

The teenage Bin Poh grew up on the nearby island of Pulau Semakau as part of a fishing family and community. But in June 1963, a British officer arrived at his home and offered an alternative career. 'They always came to our island to collect banana plants. One day they came to our place, saying "Want to become a boatman?"' he remembers. 'As a fisherman, I thought maybe there is no future for me. So I want[ed] to work in a government service.'

The teenager didn't know much about the Pulau Senang project. He knew nothing about the bold social experiment concocted by authorities in 1960 to try and reduce the overcrowding in Singapore's prisons caused by colonial efforts to curb communist insurgencies and crack down on Chinese secret societies. He knew nothing about Daniel Dutton, the idealistic British superintendent with a zealous vision of an open-air penal colony and reform through hard work, or of many of the initial inmates who arrived on Pulau Senang being former gang members, sent to the island without trial as part of the British colonial government's vision to clamp down on vice and maintain social order. 'I didn't know about what was going on down there. From far away it looked pretty nice,' he says. 'When I arrived, I soon wanted to resign. But it was too late.'

Inmates were allowed to roam free on the island but were responsible for building their own settlement. Each new arrival was given a manual task, and if Dutton deemed their behaviour satisfactory after six months, they would be reintegrated into mainland society and a government official would help them find employment.

Within the first seven months of the project, five prisoners of the original fifty were deemed worthy of release. By 1963, more than 200 had reintegrated, with the 300 inmates on the previously uninhabited island living among a self-built dining hall, sports area, kitchen, and bakery. The initial success of Pulau Senang drew international attention from a range of sociologists, UN representatives, and human rights organizations. But behind the amenities, there was a bleaker atmosphere, rife with allegations of abuse.[73] 'When I was there, the prisoners [were] all very stressed,' Bin Poh recalled. 'Because the prison warders tortured them day and night.'

According to the boatman, while staff had rotating shifts, some inmates were forced to work continuously from 3 a.m. to 6 a.m., when the tide was lowest, building a makeshift jetty from heavy stone that they would collect from the mainland. They would then return for breakfast and start their 'normal duties' lasting until the evening.

Any inmate who complained was put in what Bin Poh described as a 'small, dark house [with] no ventilation'.

When former chief minister David Marshall visited the island in 1963 he described the 'aura of fear' and conditions bordering 'on slavery'.[74] Around the same time, reports emerged that Major Peter L. James, director of the Singapore Prison Service, sent at least two directives to Dutton, requesting a scale-down of hours that often saw prisoners working throughout the night.[75]

On 12 July, something snapped.

After explosions shook Bin Poh from sleep, he opened his window to see 'that prison is burning . . . [and] around twenty or thirty prisoners approaching our barracks to find the warder.'

In his short time on the island, he had formed bonds with inmates, playing football and sneaking them cigarettes from his trips to the mainland. He believes this spared his life—the prisoners left him to grab the boat key he slept with and sound the alarm. In the meantime, inmates armed with machetes and Molotov cocktails ransacked the settlement. They eventually reached the guardhouse and set fire to the surroundings, beating Dutton with weapons after he emerged.

A testimony from a former prison warden who was the first to find Dutton's body states: 'He was burned, like a log. [Another warden had] been hacked on the forehead. The whole office was burned . . . like a war zone.'

The Pulau Senang massacre left twenty-nine injured and four prison employees dead, including Dutton. The subsequent trial, in which the court sentenced eighteen of the fifty-nine charged inmates to death, lasted sixty-four days. It was Singapore's longest and largest trial to date.

For a while, the story was the height of the headlines and the talk of the kopitiams. Then it was eclipsed by bigger news: the end of a brief shaky merger between Singapore and Malaysia and independence in 1965.

Recently, it's had a bit of a renaissance. There was the 2018 *Sisters & Senang: The Island Plays* and British journalist and political commentator, Alex Josey's book with the damning title *Pulau Senang: The Experiment that Failed*. The 2022 documentary, *Riot Island* revived the massacre in grisly reenactments. It won a series of accolades at the following year's New York Festivals TV & Film Awards. There is, as the documentary's director and producer Tom St. John Gray mentions, 'something almost Shakespearian' about Pulau Senang, 'this grand tragedy playing out on this sort of mysterious, almost mythical island.'

It's a good story. It is a story about power and violence and the breaking points of human beings. It's a story about redemption. It's a story about who we choose to make into villains. Scattered amid criticisms of Dutton as a hard-nosed slave-driver are memories of a generally fair leader, who spoke Malay and Hokkien and formed bonds with the inmates, including with Tan Kheng Ann known as 'Robert Black', the eventual ringleader of the riots.

A.N. Jenardaran, a former police officer at Pulau Senang whose statement appears in *Riot Island*, recalls a 'hardworking resourceful man.' Others said he, 'really believed you could work the evil out of anyone'. Dutton's younger half-brother Michael, who also featured in the documentary, remembers the older sibling he idolized, with his glamorous Malay wife and their work in the community, adopting children who didn't have permanent homes.

It's also a story about fear. Fear of the foreign colonial order still clinging to the last relics of power. Fear of insurgency in a period defined by reinvention and change. Fear of the people we send to an island for fear that they might corrupt us, harm us, or remind us too much of ourselves. Fear of failure that we shove to the backwaters of history.

Following the riots, Bin Poh stayed on the empty settlement, and when the prison reopened, he worked there for another four years. His commitment earned him a nautical studies certificate sponsored by the prison department. He remained in the service even after the settlement closed for good and, in 1968, was handed over from the Prisons Department to the Ministry of Interior and Defence.[76]

Pulau Senang is now a base used for military training. It's still known by its original Malay name: Pulau Senang, 'Isle of Ease'.

Sisters' Islands

Off the south coast of Singapore's mainland are the Sisters' Islands. There is Big Sister, Pulau Subar Laut, and Little Sister, Pulau Subar Darat. The shyer, younger sibling is closed to the public. Big Sister, cocky with eldest child arrogance, is open to visitors.

The water around the sisters is jade-green, freckled with the dark blots of underwater coral. The islands are now areas of marine conservation, and Laut is a hub for sea swimming and snorkelling. But once, they were two young women who loved each other, quite literally, to death.

Legend has it that Linah and Minah, the daughters of a poor widow, were close. So close that when they reached the eligible age, they refused to be married to anyone but a pair of brothers. This way, they could remain in the same family. The girls were a catch, and there was no shortage of suitors, but none of them were brothers.

Eventually, their mother died, and the young women were sent away to live with an uncle. While collecting water from a well by the sea, Linah attracted the attention of pirates who kidnapped her. Minah jumped into the water to chase after the boat, but as she approached its frantically paddling oars, a storm broke out and sucked her under the waves. Linah managed to break free and throw herself overboard to try and save her sister. The gods admired their love for each other, and as they drowned, turned them into islands, which may not have been the ideal conclusion they were hoping for, but did mean that they would get to be close to each other for all eternity.

THE HEART OF A HOME

Jon Smith

My sister is marrying an Englishman. I should have known. I should have clocked it from the day I went to visit her at Cambridge, and her Doc Martens crunched a happy skittish jazz rhythm through the sleety streets.

'Are you seeing anyone?' she asked with careful nonchalance while we cradled stocky mugs of hot chocolate. This is sister code for 'I am seeing someone.' You don't need to be a sleuth to figure this out.

His name is Jon Smith. The name of a character in a schoolbook teaching English to schoolchildren. Before Lil Sis revealed his name, I guessed it, and I did feel a bit like a sleuth then, albeit an amateur one. A laggard sleuth, who likes to clock off early by falling on the most obvious answers. I wonder how this would have looked if the positions were reversed and a white person was reeling off the most Asian names they could think of. Who says there's no advantage to being an ethnic minority?

But obviously Jon Smith is far from a two-dimensional textbook caricature. My future brother-in-law is a West Ham supporter. He is a Cambridge graduate, which is where he and Lil Sis met, and a Bromley boy. He is good-natured, clever, and always happy to have second or third helpings at family dinners, which makes him a strong hit with our mum.

Lil Sis and me, two Bad British Asians, diluting our family's Asian-ness daughter by daughter, folding ourselves further into the country that brought us up. I, too, married an Englishman. Though mine came to Asia with me.

Once upon an era in Singapore, a young Asian woman hooking up with a Caucasian man was called a Sarong Party Girl. The term comes from the sarong-wearing local girls invited to the British colonial parties to mingle with white officers. Now, it's faded to a dated jibe used to describe the women who hang around the expat clubs hungry for the perks of an exotic relationship, the dated dream of an expat package and a potential path to a new life abroad. There are other acronyms I learn, too, as I settle into the Red Dot.

LBH = loser back home. A man who is of mediocre success back in his home country but has now found his status elevated professionally and romantically by being in Asia, getting jobs and girls normally out of his league.

MBA = married but available. Self-explanatory. Not to be confused with the business qualification of the same name, though getting involved with an MBA takes a similar level of strategic planning, ruthless ambition, and hanging around offices after everyone else has left.

GCB = good class bungalow. Landed houses in posh areas of Singapore. Top prize for a single Singaporean woman is to find a Singaporean dude with a GCB, and maybe an MBA (the business kind).

We do this with relationships. We like to categorize people, especially when it comes to dating. Whether it's semi-serious acronyms or app algorithms, we try to crack the mystery of what makes us attracted to each other. It gives us a sense of control, which is comforting when it comes to something as scary as romance; it tricks us into thinking we can guess what's coming.

Amy Zhao, a PhD student at the University of Queensland, led a 2023 study exploring the effect of facial similarity on attractiveness between partners. The study covered 2,285 speed-dating interactions and concluded that 'participants . . . received higher facial attractiveness ratings from partners of the same ethnicity'.[77] When I email her to ask about this, Zhao says, 'The psychological familiarity could be a component. But overall I think that social identity definitely plays a stronger role in attraction than facial similarity.'

Growing up as an only child with no extended family in her Australian town, Zhao found that 'I didn't have many other Chinese or Asian children around me. At school, there were only one or two other Asian children in my class. And so, when it comes to dating, I have only ever dated Caucasian men. [On the other hand], I have a group of girlfriends who are Asian but were born in Australia [in areas with a larger diaspora community]. Most of them prefer to date Asian guys who grew up in Australia. So I think this speaks to the idea that people are attracted to people who have similar social upbringings to themselves.'

This is Zhao's romantic code-breaker; the mirror we hold up is internal more than external. That love is a way of solidifying your place in society, confirming where you feel you fit in.

I'm not sure I entirely agree. I've seen love cross social divides, linking people from demographics as disparate as different planets. I believe love is a thousand anomalies, a million glitches in the matrix. It is something we will still refuse to give up on and try and rationalize, codify, and understand, probably until the end of time. But I also believe that love is belonging, outside society's confines. Love shows you who you are beyond ethnic and social identities, *in spite* of ethnic and social identities. Love is home.

Mooncakes

There isn't much farming in Singapore, but we celebrate the end of harvest. We fill the malls and parks with bulbous cheerful lanterns, glowing avatars of happy families, and gold ingots. For two weeks, everyone eats mooncakes, even those who don't like mooncakes. It's hard not to like mooncakes though. There are so many kinds. The traditional ones are a clash of sweet lotus or red bean paste around a sunny orb of salty cured egg yolk. Some contain a speckled mosaic of dried fruit and nuts. Some have sausage. The hotels and bakeries are becoming more inventive, swapping the classic pastry casing for sticky mochi skin or stamping the tops with their favourite Sanrio characters. Mid-Autumn Festival is a mooncake rat-race, everyone vying to bake the best one.

What in Britain was a niche kitsch event confined mostly to Chinatown, is here, a nation-wide celebration. Paul and I wander among the spindly, glowing branches of the Supertree Grove in Gardens by the Bay and watch an open-air performance of Cantonese opera that neither of us understands a word of.

It strikes me, not for the first time, how much I love this man sitting awkwardly cross-legged among fidgety Chinese schoolchildren, humming along happily to a completely alien tune in a completely alien language. Love surprises you. It sneaks up at unexpected moments in the B-roll of the everyday or in a mosquito-speckled field in front of warblers in period costume. Love is built from a million mundane moments. Love is remembering a joke you shared, or not even the joke, but the way it felt to be light and giddy and silly together, smirking to yourself on a random street like a lunatic with a secret lottery-winning ticket.

Behind the mooncakes, Mid-Autumn Festival is a love story. The prolific archer Hou Yi, centuries ago, saved the community by shooting down nine of the ten suns that were scorching their crops. Hou Yi had everything—a successful hunting career, a beautiful wife, Chang-E, and now, as thanks for saving the village from starvation, a gift from the gods, a small bottle of immortality elixir.

But, as is often the case in these legends, the good fortune didn't last long. And, as is also troublingly common in such legends, its undoing was due to a woman. Hou Yi asked Chang-E to hide the elixir in a safe place in the house and went about his heroic business. Some versions of the story say he hid the bottle's ingredients from her and curiosity drove her to take a sip. Others give her credit for swallowing the elixir to protect it from a thieving enemy who approached the house. Still others say that Hou Yi was having an affair, and Chang-E chugged the elixir as a vengeful parting shot. In any case, by the time the archer returned, the elixir was gone and so was his wife.

Chang-E had been sent to the moon, where she was to live forever, immortal but alone. A devastated Hou Yi set up a table of fruits and perfectly round mooncakes to remember his wife and hope that, one day, they might meet again. In my favourite versions of the story, the gods take pity on him and allow the couple to reunite every Mid-Autumn Festival, when the moon is brightest.

Reunion runs strong throughout the Mid-Autumn Festival. Couples who normally live apart at their respective family homes launch shared wishes inside homemade lanterns. Families get together for celebratory meals around dishes of duck and hairy crab. Relatives who live parallel lives in the same city, cross tracks for one short week, aligning briefly like a chance meeting between former lovers or a full moon in September.

Lessons on Love Learned up a Mountain

It's our fifth anniversary and I am up a mountain. The air is thin, not enough to be a health hazard but enough to make an otherwise healthy couple in their thirties wheeze and trudge like pugs with a chronic smoking addiction. The track is scattered with boulders, bulbous and slippery smooth as exercise balls.

This is what you get when you say, 'I do,' for better or worse, for richer or poorer, in sickness, health, or mud-splattered insanity.

This is what you get when you fall in love with a small-city Essex boy who thinks he's David Attenborough.

Mount Kinabalu is, according to travel websites, not a challenging climb, 'but by no means a walk in the park'. This made sense when I read it. There weren't many parks I knew of that had a peak altitude of 4,095 metres. We planned our training schedules. I stopped taking the elevator and started using the stairs. We did a last-minute panic shop at Kinabalu City's branch of Decathlon; a grape purple waterproof jacket and one hiking pole between us two. Marriage means sharing everything, right?

On our first day, I realize how right these websites are. Mount Kinabalu is not a walk in the park. It is a million times better; muddy paths splattered with morning sunlight, craggy cliff faces that spit skinny waterfalls into mumbling creeks, and a background of sloping gorges of silver rock covered with a carpet of bulbous tree heads like broccoli tops. Beauty like a gut punch, views so starkly stunning they rob you of whatever breath you have left.

'Look! A mountain squirrel!' I squeak excitedly to Paul.

'We've done the first kilometre in under an hour!' Paul chirps back, equally excited. Here I learn the first thing about marriage from hiking up a mountain on your anniversary. There will always be one of you steadfastly planning your journey and one of you pointing out random sights along the way. It's probably better if the first person manages directions.

There are three of us in this marriage: Paul, me, and our personal romantic interloper, a guide called Pis ('pronounced like Peace', he informs us). Pis is twenty-five. 'So old! Too old!,' he laments as he skips up the crags in flip-flops. I try to rebut this complaint, but my extra decade and years of living in polluted cities have me panting past any lengthy discourse. Pis is a local Kinabaluan, the youngest of six and an excellent hiker, though he says he doesn't really like hiking. What Pis really likes is rap music, especially our own London boy, Central Cee.

'Wagwan!' Pis calls cheerily to the fellow guides as we dodge roots and duck branches. 'These are my brothers!'

We pass a lot of these brothers and their tourist charges: various British, American, and Europeans in various states of exhaustion. The national park limits visiting climbers to 163 a day, but in 2021 around 129,208 tourists attempted the trek up the world's third-highest island peak, with numbers estimated at even higher since then.[78] There aren't any statistics on how many were marking marital milestones. I learn the second thing about marriage from hiking on your anniversary, you are never really alone. There will always be other couples who seem to be faster or slower, more in tune or more unaligned when it comes to ticking the boxes of successful happy married life. Ignore them and share something private and intimate, like a squished pack of Oreos.

Lesson three on marriage from hiking up a mountain: nothing like an Oreo to make something better.

The clouds break as we cross a narrow bridge, shooting blades of light down a plunging ravine.

That afternoon, it starts to rain. Trails turn into boulders, and as the canary-yellow walls of our lodge appear in the drizzly distance, my legs decide they've had enough. I shuffle grumpily with the speed of a tortoise navigating rush hour traffic. Paul—multiple times fitter and faster—shuffles along with me, offering encouragement through mouthfuls of Oreo crumbs.

'It'll get easier. It'll be easier on the way down,' he promises, and somehow, I believe him and we make it to shelter.

Our home for the night is an eco-lodge, which means we are warm with the smugness of sustainable tourism but cold from the lack of hot water. Departure time for the second day is 1.30 a.m., so the fittest and fastest among us has a chance of reaching the peak at sunrise. Have you ever clung to the sheer cliff of a rock face, lit by the firefly glow of twenty hiking headlamps? Neither have I, until I find myself entangled, both matrimonially and by the frayed rope we are gripping for balance, with my husband.

We scoot up the slate sheets on our knees and buttocks. The sky above the pinprick lights of the city is streaked with faint brushstrokes of pink and tangerine.

I tell Paul to stop matching his faster pace to my crawl and to go on ahead. Sunrise is threatening to outpace us, and while I don't have a realistic chance of reaching the peak in time, he does. Some people get funny when I tell this bit, but this is my next lesson about marriage when hiking up a mountain: love is walking step by step, but it's also giving the person you love the space and energy to occasionally go on ahead. It's celebrating the wins, whether you achieve them together or separately. It's spurring each other on, especially when the little bastard is off like a rocket, his headlamp bounding like a firefly across the plains.

Besides, I have Pis. We joke and chat and practise hip-hop moves on slanting slate plains. As the last smears of sunrise turn the sky from grey to dirty blue, we reach the summit. There is a sign confirming we have indeed climbed 4,095 metres, but more importantly, there is a hug. It's sweaty and anorak-clad, but through the synthetic fabric is the comforting warmth, smell, and muffled heartbeat that's accompanied me across continents, through five years of marriage and now up a mountain.

We start our descent, and here's my next hiking-related marriage lesson: people lie. Going down is not easier. Boulders that were tough to climb up are round, slippery gobstoppers of slime that present no other option but to shimmy on your behind. I tear the seat of my leggings and for a while, the hiking community of west Sabah is treated to a view of my anniversary underwear, a sensible pair of Marks and Spencer's cotton briefs. We forget our sole hiking pole at a toilet stop.

Lesson number six: marriage is sharing everything except hiking poles.

This time it's Paul's knees which buckle, Paul who struggles and lags behind. I give chipper words of comfort while shuffling my increasingly exposed rear over fallen logs. 'It'll get easier near the bottom,' I promise. 'It'll be easier in a few hours when we're stuffing our face with pasta.' Somehow, he believes me, and we make it to the finish line, limping and triumphant and hungry.

There's no manual to marriage that you can find up a mountain. People don't hike Kinabalu to embark on some form of eco-based nuptial training. They do it for the experience, the unique romantic feeling of sharing something beautiful, hard, unpredictable, and precious together.

We spend the next day sitting on the beach watching the waves toss surfers over foam-tipped peaks. We are sitting because our muscles won't let us stand. The sound of the waves mingles with our whinging.

'I can't believe we did that,' we murmur. 'Never again.'

'Let's plan our next one!' Paul says two weeks after we return. We have learned nothing.

My Grandmother's House

My paternal grandmother, Mook Leng's house, is a bungalow on a quiet Melbourne street. A twenty-minute drive from the city centre. Easy access to good neighbourhood schools. A green park with a playground and air that smells like eucalyptus. These are the things the estate agent said on the brochure, though they're not of any interest to my gran, who rarely goes into the city and whose youngest son has been battling a slowly growing bald spot that crept up on him a few months ago.

'Put some sun cream on it,' teases Mum, poking at the pink sphere from the front passenger seat. Dad bats her away with one hand while turning the steering wheel into the suburbs.

The bungalow is divided into three parts: the front, the middle, and the back. It starts with an open sitting room with a sofa, my grandma Mook Leng's La-Z-Boy recliner chair, and a large flat screen TV, which alternates between CNN and Cantonese dramas. When Aunt Elsie's son Davin visits from the States with his twins, it takes a detour into cartoons. There is a Christmas tree at Christmas and a permanent porcelain model of the Chinese god of longevity, Shoulao, clutching his peach and staff from his vantage point on the mantelpiece.

At the back are my older cousins' childhood bedrooms, where Lil Sis and I would sleep when we stayed over, squished together in one bed. There is also a lounge where on family occasions, the cousin could gather to watch movies or pummel each other to smithereens on Street Fighter.

There is also a door that leads out to one of my grandmother's two pride and joys. One is the front yard, where an orchestra of western roses fluff their petals like debutantes. The other is the backyard, where the air smells like woodchips and the soil is splattered with a sea of crimson chillies. This is where my cousin Garrett and I dug mud traps for our younger siblings. It's where my grandmother strains her knees with hours of tending and trimming and pruning. When I help her, she peppers her work with anecdotes about her three children growing up, grumbling casual criticisms with affection.

'Your aunt Elsie, such a temper she had! So angry, I was almost scared!'

'Your aunt Zanie, always running round, biting more than she can chew. Once, she ate so much durian in one go, she made herself sick. Vomited all over my carpet. So hard to get the smell out!'

'Your daddy, so fussy. Once, when he was little, he only ate chicken and egg for a month!'

The middle part of the house is its heart and stomach. People say Asian houses smell of Asian food, like it's a bad thing, like the wafting smell of curry, juicy chicken thighs marinated in tangerine spices then stewed for hours isn't a scent of care and love. The kitchen is where my grandmother taught us to pound chillies. It is where she bought bamboo mats and salmon from the local market and taught us how to mould squishy sushi rolls, and where she made *zok* rice congee when we were ill.

This is where, at Christmas and Chinese New Year, we assemble a makeshift fold-up table and plastic chairs: the 'kids' table', where the younger generation sits, even though the youngest of us (Lil Sis) is over thirty and some of us have kids of our own. We pass dishes back and forth between here and the 'adults' table' in the adjoining dining room with fabric seated, wood-backed chairs round the table topped with a sluggishly rotating Lazy Susan. It's a rotating stage of potluck, everyone brings their best dish, hoping to nourish but also outshine other family members. My aunty Elsie's plump and delicious curry puffs. My aunt Zanie's cookies, intricately etched with icing. My cousin Serena's fluffy durian ice-cream dessert.

Mum prepares her own specialty: Shanghainese basted pork shank and baby bok choy. She cooks it for hours in soy sauce, wine, and insecurity. 'Those Malaysian-Chinese never appreciate good Shanghainese food,' she gripes, over rich, salty steam.

Home is more than just a structure; it's an extension of who we are—we showcase our dreams and fears along with the furniture or hide them away like dirty laundry when guests come round.

This house is full of memories, good and bad, tangled together like the heap of shoes lying on the doormat when the family descends.

My dad is the ultimate prodigal son; he retired back to Melbourne years ago, on the basis that with Brexit and his children grown, there wasn't anything left for him in the UK. Leaving his family and home to reconnect with his roots. When I watch him sitting on the cream cushions of my grandmother's faux-leather sofa, speaking in quiet cautious Cantonese, it is as if he's had thirty years shaved off him and is the shy, recent graduate about to leave Australia for his first international posting. This is what happens when you come home, a part of you reverts back to who you were before you left.

Lil Sis and I don't really get the concept of 'home'. Not in the way our friends seem to, in that very British 'an Englishman's home is his castle' kind of way. We've moved homes more times than we can count, within countries, in different countries, from when I was born in a small apartment in Tokyo to London's Chiswick, Japan, Australia, Singapore, back to London, each home completely different, the only commonality is the people living in its rooms. Lil Sis came to me bewildered once, after comforting a friend moved to tears by moving out of her childhood home.

'I felt for her, but I couldn't empathize,' she said. 'It's just a load of cardboard boxes.'

The author Megan Harlan documents her similarly itinerant childhood in her book, *Mobile Home.*

'During all my travels, as each of my homes was replaced by another, again another . . . the world loosened for me into flexible components; the view from another kitchen window, shadows cast by unfamiliar trees . . . real life kept disappearing on me. This ongoing abstraction was abetted because we lived mostly out of boxes; boxes in various states of being packed and unpacked, sealed up, sliced open, carted off to moving vans . . . sitting in my new strange-smelling bedroom.'

It's just a load of cardboard boxes. It's so much more than a load of cardboard boxes.

So, our grandmother's house is the closest we'll ever get to crossing this elusive threshold of a 'permanent home'. Every third Christmas, or the occasional random Lunar New Year, it is there as we pull up jetlagged, slightly nervous, ready to replug ourselves into a temporary life we've put on pause, solid and welcoming even in the absence of a kitsch doormat. Even the glossiest estate agent's brochures don't talk about this.

The Houses Before My Grandmother's House

My grandma Mook Leng's house was not always my grandma's house. First, her house was on a rubber plantation in Malaysia, where she lived with her mother and siblings, while her father ran a business in a different house, on a different part of this empire of trees. Her father sold rubber, with a side business in opium. The air on the plantation smelt like burnt tyres. Once, he came to visit and she cried and hid from this strange man offering her western biscuits.

When the war sirens came closer, they cut her hair short. Young girls were being kidnapped and raped, they said. Her aunt made her a vest, heavy with the family's jewellery sewn into the linings.

Later, her house was a comfortable modern townhouse in Kuala Lumpur, the capital of a newly formed federation. It was a full house, full of promises and potential and business deals, as my grandfather started a new bank in a burgeoning finance landscape. Full of children as she started their family, the doctors cutting her open to release my dad the same year that crowds gathered in Freedom Square to shouts of 'Merdeka' and the birth of a new independent Malaya.

When my grandparents' marriage broke down, my father and his sisters went away to boarding school and university in Melbourne. The rooms were empty and foggy with the dreamy numbness of barbiturates, hours skating smoothly into days and weeks and years.

She eventually moved to Australia to be closer to her children. A home is more than just a building; it's the people in it, the people near it. A 2019 study by the University of Queensland examined the importance of home-building on older generations of Australian Chinese immigrants.[79] It found that although a place of residence anchored a geographical sense of home, the feeling of 'being at home' was triggered by the proximity of social and family relations.

My grandma Mook Leng doesn't miss Malaysia. There's nothing left for her there, nothing to miss. She's Australian now, she says, and has been for over thirty years. When I ask her about her past, which I wring out of her in a mixture of Cantonese, English, and broken Mandarin, she shakes it off. 'My story *bu hao ting*,' she says dismissively. 'Not pretty to listen to.'

Home can be a sanctuary. Home can be a haven. But sometimes home is a shell of bad memories, a skin you can't wait to shed. You move onwards and upwards, a new house, new life, each one different but hopefully a little better than the last.

An Ugly Love Story

There was a tram that ferried teenaged Mook Leng to her weekend job at the local cinema's box office. The doors would open, and he would be sitting in one of the front seats, well-dressed and good-looking, watching her as she walked down the aisle. He was the son of a rubber plantation owner—they had that smelly rich business in common—and his father had sent his younger brothers abroad to study while he, the eldest son, stayed at home to take care of business. He was exciting and ambitious. He rode the tram but owned a car, an MG Sports model with bug-eyed headlights and clean rubber tyres. His name was Oon Seng Tiong, but as the British clawed back their influence in the new Malayan Union, some people knew him as Jeffrey.

'I was with someone else at the time,' my grandmother remembers. 'But when I met him, I soon forgot this other guy.' She still can't remember the name of this former boyfriend. My grandfather eclipsed the memory of anyone before him.

Later, people warned her. Telok Anson was a small town, and Sieng Tong Jeffrey had a reputation as a playboy, a man who was careless with people's hearts and went through relationships like business deals. But this just made him more exciting to my grandmother, and my grandfather was persistent. He went to her family to negotiate. This was different, he said. He wanted to get married and Mook Leng—poor, uneducated, smart, beautiful—was the person he wanted to marry.

The wedding took place in the lobby of a modern hotel in the city. There's a black-and-white photo of the couple, my grandmother grinning and wrapped in western lace, my grandfather slick-haired and smiling as he cleaves a knife through a five-tier cake, ready to start his early thirties as a married man. She was nineteen years old.

They moved to the city to chase business. Their house was in the unfashionable Cheras outskirts, but it was modern and clean, a family home. My grandmother had her three children, and as the scars on her C-section healed, my grandfather did business. He bet on horses at the racecourse. He spent late evenings in a private club in the city. One of the hostesses there caught his eye. She was young and attentive. She was poor, uneducated, smart, beautiful.

My grandfather's evenings got later. He booked an extra ticket on a business trip to Europe. Clichés become clichés because they're tired, recognizable, and keep happening. Someone told my grandmother he was having an affair. It was a courtesy, an airing of something everyone already knew.

She went to the doctor and got pills. They were fresh rubber white and in neat rows like smiling teeth. They made the days go fast but she floated slowly, like she was walking underwater.

She headed upwards, onwards and outwards, fraying and unravelling at the edges. She drove out of the city up to the peak of Mount Ulu Kali. The Genting Highlands were also in the midst of reinventing themselves. A few years ago, Lim Goh Tong, a South Chinese entrepreneur rich from the heavy machine industry, had launched a mountaintop resort, a quick weekend getaway from the pressures of the city. When it opened in 1971, Tunku Abdul Rahman had granted the Genting Highlands the only casino licence in the country. 'I had fallen head over heels in love with this virgin wilderness and vowed to transform it into my dream resort,' Lim had said.

In this spruced up virgin wilderness, she learned to play Blackjack and Sic Bo, and even three-card poker, but her favourite was Roulette. You could choose your level of risk, red or black, straddle your chip across an entire row of possible futures or place it boldly backing just one square. Once the wheel started, all bets were off. Your fate was out of your control, spun by a well-dressed stranger.

A friend introduced her to a lawyer who turned up at her door with papers, and they covered the table in official looking black and white. My grandmother watched the words lying across the pages like sleeping beetles.

She told the lawyer she'd never learned to read.

They started again. The lawyer recited each page aloud, slowing proudly over each particularly complicated legal term. She stopped him on a phrase she recognized, 'joint ownership'. There was no sharing left in her anymore. The lawyer went away and returned with new papers. The house she once hated was hers.

Fathers on Fathers

When my dad was young, family time started on Friday evenings. My grandmother would assemble her three children, freshly washed and dressed in their best clothes, in an army line behind the door.

'Get ready to welcome your father,' she would hiss. My grandfather's car would purr into the driveway. They would hear his weight against the door. And then they would welcome him.

Jeffrey Sieng Tong Oon had ventured into finance. It was a period of potential. The first central bank had been founded in 1959 and had sowed the seeds for a fertile home-grown banking industry to grow over the next decade. My grandfather would spend weekdays in the office, with his second family, or at the races. On the weekends, he would come home.

'There was always the best food on Friday evenings,' my dad remembers. 'It was like she was trying to remind him of what he had given up. And we were always on our best behaviour. It was important to my mum, I knew that, even at that age'

We are marching through mud along the banks of the Yarra River, my parents' French bulldog in tow. I am talking to my father about fathers, our steps perfectly in tandem, apart from when the skittish pull of the lead sends me into drunken zigzags.

After dinner, the family would cluster around the television. 'We'd watch all kinds of things, *Star Trek*, *Batman*, *Mister Ed*, and *I Love Lucy*. There was a really inappropriate show called *The Black and White Minstrel Show*, where white actors would dress up in blackface. All the parents loved it.' My grandfather also loved chocolates. A flurry of discarded wrappers would gather around the house when he was around. And he loved smoking too. 'But,' my dad says, 'he stopped when we were born. That's how he showed us he loved us.'

There were other ways he showed love too. Whatever new childhood trend gripped my dad's fascination, it became my grandfather's sole mission to track it down. There were presents, miniature model tanks, and perfect replicas of military aircraft. One day, my father came home from school and found a makeshift badminton court set up in the living room. 'There were court lines and lights and everything,' remembers my dad.

They played all evening, the shuttlecocks bouncing off the sharp corners of the furniture.

School was split into two sessions, morning and afternoon. When he was in the morning session, my dad would sometimes travel to his father's office after class, a large office block among the colonial art deco buildings and modern oblong squares of the city. My grandfather had a spacious side office and the walk would stretch through the open-air workspace, flanks of silent eyes staring as the general manager's son scuttled shyly through rows of desks and silent questions.

My grandfather would always be in the middle of something important when his son arrived. My dad would stand in front of his desk, waiting in silence, sometimes over half an hour, until my grandfather would raise his head, and then they would go for lunch.

Men talk about becoming fathers. They write poems about it: W. B. Yeats' 'A Prayer for my Daughter', Robert Yeo's 'A Dragon for the Family'. They write philosophical essays on it: Montaigne's 'On the Affection of Fathers for Their Children'. For a gender widely stereotyped as the 'silent sex', fatherhood is the thing that flicks the switch. Sometimes they reflect on how their own fathers have shaped them and their own experience of parenthood—an infinity mirror hall of fathers, generations of paternal influence staring back at you.

There's no shortage of absent fathers in the almanac of parenthood either. Buddha disappearing under night's darkness in search of enlightenment while his wife and young son slept. The Vietnamese folktale of a 'Shadow of the Absent Father'. Darth Vader's heavy, helmeted breathing as he topples away from Luke Skywalker.

But what if your father is neither absent nor present but treading that purgatory in between?

My father's father was a provider, a gift-giver, a semi-stranger who'd turn up on Friday evenings, change out of the clothes and who he'd been during the week, and be a family man for a weekend or a Lunar New Year holiday. When he left, my dad remembers the mornings my grandmother didn't get out of bed, the way she'd move groggily through the house, as if she were sleepwalking.

Eventually, he left, too, for a boarding school in Melbourne where he sat in classrooms of pink faces, where the only other student of colour was a curly-haired son of a Stolen Generation. The weekend father figure faded from his mind.

The soil on the riverbank is rusty red. It sticks to our shoes in clumps. 'I think when you're a man, your father is your first role model,' muses my dad. 'I think for me, my dad became an anti-role model. Everything about his approach to family, I've tried to do the opposite.'

My grandfather Jeffrey died shortly after my sister was born. There's a family photo from a few months before, staged and solemn. He's in the centre, Lil Sis on his knee, looking serious and surprised as if he never quite expected to still have all these people around.

When he lay in a Kuala Lumpur hospital, all three of his children flew in from Australia. My grandmother came too. She took his hand. She called him '老友', 'old friend'. She was on her best behaviour for one last time, one gentle goodbye, one final portrait of a family man.

Bathing Buddha

In Chinatown, there is a temple dedicated to a tooth. Not teeth, you understand. Not the veneration of dentures in general. This temple has found its chopper of choice, and it's baring it to the world.

The Buddha Tooth Relic Temple and Museum was built in 2007 to house the ancient canine recovered from Buddha's funeral pyre in Kushinagar. The building is beautiful—tiers of elegant arching gables sprout from frames of a deep raspberry red. Their peaks shelter a quiet roof garden where a whirring prayer wheel spins like a vinyl record amid leafy palms and red ginger flowers. The design is based on Tang dynasty architecture and the Buddhist mandala, a microcosm of the eternal universe. Inside, the air buzzes with murmuring chants of orange-robed monks under high ceilings of a sea of glass lanterns.

On the top floor, the holy fang sits inside an elaborate gold stupa. According to temple lore, the tooth was discovered by an abbot in Myanmar in 1980, who kept the discovery quiet until 2002, when he handed it over to a monk from Singapore's Golden Pagoda Temple shortly before he died. The monk, Shi Fa Zhao decided a new temple worthy of sole veneration of the tooth needed to be built and the site was secured in 2005.

The tooth is broad, flat-topped, long as a baby elephant's tusk. While most of Buddha was cremated after he died, a few relics were spread across select teachers worldwide as a way of passing on his holy teachings, like intimate family heirlooms.

I am here for Vesak Day, the most important festival in the Buddhist calendar, marking the May full moon when Buddha was born, died, and attained enlightenment.

The entrance of the temple is crowded. People mingle under a scented cloud of incense. They hold joss sticks and offer flowers and hold candles like lighters at a rock concert. We have come to bathe Buddha on his birthday. On a small altar in the middle of the lobby, a line of people is waiting to ladle water over a small, plump, chalk-white model of Buddha, one arm raised in a decent imitation of Travolta's *Saturday Night Fever.*

'We don't bathe the Buddha because he got dirty,' Kathy, a cheerful volunteer with the Buddhist Library, tells me later. She is wearing a gold necklace with a tiny baby-faced Buddha dangling cross-legged from the chain. 'It's a way of washing off our bad thoughts, our irritation, reminding ourselves what we actually need to be happy, which isn't very much.'

Growing up as Prince Siddhartha, the young Buddha had everything. All the riches in the kingdom, a beautiful wife and baby boy, and a father who loved him so dearly he cushioned him from seeing any misfortune for fear his son would be moved to leave and fulfil his birth prophecy of becoming a great healer. King Śuddhodana—Asia's first helicopter parent.

But the king's ill thought out plan didn't work. The restless prince came across an old man on one of his walks outside the palace walls and was shocked that such tired frailty of life could exist. Then, he saw a man wracked by illness. Then, a dead body being carried through the streets, and finally, a homeless religious ascetic. He was so moved by compassion and fear of his own vulnerability to age, illness, and death, he decided the only thing he could do was leave through a window in the middle of the night, walking away from his sleeping wife and son, to seek life's ultimate meaning as an ascetic himself. The rest is history. So much history. Centuries and centuries of it, panels painting the walls of temples, gold and gilded models of Buddha in front of me. Buddha touching the earth to signify his attainment of enlightenment. Buddha cross-legged. Buddha reclining serenely on his right elbow, about to enter the state of nirvana.

On Vesak Day, you bathe Buddha three times, once for his birth as an ordinary human boy, once for his rebirth as an enlightened being, and once for his death at eighty, triggered, according to some, by a dish of wild mushrooms.

I'm looking at a panel describing Mara's attack. It's a well-known story, beginner level Buddhism. The demon Mara tried to interrupt Siddhartha's quest for ultimate wisdom with a crowd of beautiful women. These female sirens, sometimes said to be Mara's daughters, and their Lord of Death dad descended on the prince, seeping under his skin, trying to seduce him, pulling him down with jealousy, frustration, boredom, temptation, shame. We've all felt the weight of these things, we know their heaviness.

My favourite part about that story is the general consensus that Siddhartha struggled. Not because I'm a sadist but because it gels with what many Buddhists have told me is one of the central tenets of Buddhism, that Buddha was a human being, like us—flawed, imperfect, subject to grief, cravings, insecurities. And yes, he reached inner peace, but after trial and error and an exhaustingly long time. He eventually realized the life of ascetic self-punishment wasn't the way to divine happiness after all and, instead, turned to the arguably equally tough task of achieving complete inner peace with himself, his past lives, and acceptance of his current circumstances. As Kathy of the Buddha necklace puts it, 'Buddhism's a bit like pop psychology. You have to do the work.'

Eventually, the now-enlightened Siddhartha returned to his family of origin. I wonder what the young prince Rahula, then around twelve years old, must have thought about his father's sudden return as this metamorphosed monk. Ever the savvy pre-teen, the first thing he apparently asked his prodigal parent was for his inheritance. By that point, the Buddha formerly known as Prince had lost all his gold and riches, but he gave the boy the most valuable thing he had. He dedicated his time to teaching Rahula everything he had learned in his travels around the world. How to find happiness in the simplest of things. How to drown out the sounds of your demons.

The boy behind me is about seven years old. His father is trying to guide his arm, teaching him how to manoeuvre the ladle. 'Lift it up to the shoulders. Yeah, like that, don't splash.'

The kid looks at him sceptically. He's just old enough to ask himself if Dad's deity ladling expertise is really all that. Then, after a moment, he extends a hand, and the two of them lift the spoon. Water splashes down Buddha's chubby torso. Washing off yesterday's demons. Ready to get up and try again. Together.

Kali

The colours in Little India are like a cheerful slap in the face. I am wading through blushing mangoes from fruit carts, steely silvers from jewellery shops, and garlands of sunset orange mala flowers swinging lazily from hooks. At an outdoor café, a diner eats prata in front of a mural of a man making prata. I walk past the eyeball-white sign promising 'face bleeching'. I worm my way down crooked streets and the *pintu pagar* swinging doors of merchant Tan Teng Niah's rainbow house, the last surviving Chinese villa in Little India.

Today is Lord Murugan's birthday, and I never turn down the invitation to a birthday party, even if the birthday party in question is for a six-faced Hindu god you've never met. So, here I am, in front of one of the oldest Hindu temples in Singapore.

Asian etiquette suggests you take off your shoes before entering someone's house. In the case of this house, there is also a sign telling you in no uncertain terms to do so.

I extract myself from my sandals and step inside.

There are around 200,000 practising Hindus in Singapore. Most are made up from the waves of Tamil labourers who arrived from South India in the nineteenth century under the British East India company. Places of worship have a way of becoming centrepieces of small societies and Sri Veeramakaliamman started as a simple shrine in 1855, then a wooden temple. Then, they called it 'Temple of the Lime Village' after the local lime pits and their workers who built the shrine.

Now, layers upon layers of brightly-coloured figures rise from the underworld to the heavens. Pot-bellied guardians and topaz monkey gods play against Dali-esque murals. There are shrines, chubby cherubic plaster babies, and a door with rows of miniature doorbells so you can ring in your entrance and your exit.

The original founders of the temple were so worried about the hostility they'd face in their new home country that they devoted the temple to the scariest, deadliest deity they could find.

This is the goddess Kali, or more specifically, Kali the Fearless. Kali is a complex deity. A blue-faced, sharp-tongued deity of death, and the wife of Lord Shiva, she was originally associated with sexuality, violence, and trampling those who cross her. She is decked with her garland of skulls said to represent the destruction of false egos and pretences we spin ourselves. Then, in later centuries, she became linked to the concept of motherly love and around the twentieth century, to female empowerment.[80] 'Paradoxically,' says the Encyclopaedia Britannica website, as if motherhood exempts you from things like death, or sexuality. As if motherhood doesn't come with a protective rage that is almost primal.

Different eras of Kali are stationed around the temple grounds. Kali, straggle-haired and blue-skinned in a halo of flames, dressed in only a garland of skulls and a belt of severed heads, her tongue sticking out of a blood-rimmed mouth. Kali, doe-eyed and regal, her four arms juggling different tools of compassion, destruction, and disillusion. Kali trampling her husband under her feet, Kali, in the form of Parvati, tenderly nurturing her two sons, Ganesha and Murugan. Visitors take small tear-shaped ghee lamps to lay at the altars of each Kali and touch a fingerful of fine ash to their foreheads, leaving a soot-coloured *bindi* or *tilak* on their foreheads. No matter how destructive, how vicious, how submissive, there is a nod of quiet recognition for all Kalis here.

At the back of the temple, there is an annexe. It clashes with the busy noise and colours of the rest of the complex. This room is clean and airy, with the feel of a classroom kept for extracurricular activities. The floor is decked with mats where people congregate to eat floury ghee balls and puddles of curried rice, dished out by two volunteers at the entrance.

Sitting on these rattan mats, chewing mouthfuls of flame-coloured rice with strangers, I meet Mega and Sudasa, shy teenagers who moved here from Tamil Nadu three months ago to work as porters. I speak with soft-spoken Bala who has grown up in Little India and runs a textiles business that sells jewelled saris, who is here because it is a Thursday, and Thursdays are auspicious days for Guru, his zodiac god. I sit by office worker Aashna, who doesn't tell me where she's from, but quietly and insistently pushes more ghee balls onto my plate.

I make a plateful of faux pas, which starts with me using both hands, and ends with me spilling ghee and rice down my shorts, but my new friends pretend not to notice. There's something sort of familial about that, letting someone make messy mistakes, over and over again, waiting patiently until we sort it out ourselves.

Shashti, a chipper, wizened temple volunteer takes me to a simmering cauldron. In it, he's mixing black sugar, milk, and the thick fibres of mango pulp. This, he tells me, is for the bathing of Shiva. After that, the remainder will be shared around the congregation.

There are drums signalling the start of Shiva's bathtime, along with a *nadaswaram*, a flare-ended tasselled wind instrument that sounds a bit like an oboe, if an oboe could grab you by the stomach and shake your insides with its deep, throaty sound. Bathing deities is a cross-creed trend. Cleanliness and godliness are as much of a partnership as soap and water. But unlike the Buddha Tooth Relic Temple and Museum, where the devotees filed in orderly lines and the only background sound was the low-level chanting of tangerine-robed monks, here there is music, chaos, and people sitting haphazardly on the floor to watch the ceremony or jostling to take photos, as if Shiva is some sort of super-influencer, which of course, in some sense, he is.

The bathing ritual here is called *abhishekam*, and it starts with a bucket of coconut water. Then, a fountain of creamy milk. Then honey, then thick, snowy curd, covering the deity with a coat of yoghurt-y sheepskin. Each wash represents a different wish: water for energy, milk for purity and illumination, curd for prosperity. We're wishing these things unto Shiva but we're also wishing them for ourselves.

As he undergoes this waterboarding of blessings and desires, Shiva's wife watches him from around the main hall in all her guises.

We like to define ourselves by neat labels: mother, warrior, wife. It's a nifty shortcut to remind others, and us, of who we are. In a world where technological and medical advances have multiplied our options, we like to define ourselves by our choices too. 'We choose motherhood,' said American writer Nora Ephron. But sometimes we don't. Sometimes we can't. Sometimes we spill over the sides of our cleverly defined boxes like toddlers colouring outside the lines. Sometimes, like an abhishekam bath, life is messy.

Kali looks like a woman who has it all, and not in the way you might expect of, say, Beyoncé. She is calm and flawed and angry. She's a mother and a demon warrior. She's a wife but occasionally stamps her husband under her demon foot. She's all of these things, sometimes all at once.

As I leave the temple, ringing out my exit as I go, someone has kicked my shoes around. They're lying haphazardly across the damp tiles, splayed in different directions. They look like they're exactly where they're meant to be.

Bugis Street

Bugis Street used to be the place where people went to set their bums on fire. The Dance of the Flaming Arseholes, they called it, and people sure danced. They danced as if there was chilli in their veins. They danced like their arses were alight.

This area used to be a popular fifties and sixties watering hole for the visiting army officers and sailors with a heady network of cheap alcohol, local street snacks, and the city's transgender population enjoying an underground respite from the city-state's conservative culture. A popular ritual for the servicemen was to stick a roll of paper where the sun don't shine, light it, and boogie until the sun came up, or the flames petered out.

To what extent these waving buttocks caught on, or caught alight, is not heavily documented, unlike the paper-stuffed orifices themselves.

Before that, the area around Bugis Street was a pre-war hub for Japanese brothels, and before that a place where migrant communities used to work and live during the time of Singapore's founding. The name possibly comes from the Bugis Sulawesi maritime traders who travelled and settled down in various parts of Southeast Asia.[81] Now though, Bugis has cleaned up its act. Like an ageing rockstar putting down his drumsticks and taking up his reading glasses, the burning bums and public toilets have given way to the wide white aisles of another shopping mall. The cheap boozers have ceded to Atlas, an imposing art deco monolith regularly boasting a spot on lists for the best bars in the world. Kampong Glam, named after the popular wood used for boat-making once found in the local area, is now a hub of tourist shops, tattoo parlours, and cafés, flanked by the colourful murals of Haji Lane.

Bugis has grown up, spruced up, but you can still feel the thumping pulse of history, like the bass beat of a song you can't forget, pulsing under its skin.

Abdullah

Near Haji Lane is the tilted minaret of the Hajjah Fatimah Mosque. A travel blog I read somewhere described it as 'Singapore's Leaning Tower of Pisa'. The minaret's spire, pointing wonkily upwards, is gothic and slender, like that of a European church. The interior is framed with traditional Malay carvings. Different cultures, clashing together under one religion. 'My great-grandfather travelled a lot and drew influence from his travels,' says Abdullah, the current mosque guardian. 'If you look, it doesn't look like an Arab mosque at all!'

Hajjah Fatimah, the wealthy merchant from Malacca who married a Bugis prince, settled into the Kampong Glam area and helped build the area up through her philanthropy, contributing funds towards housing initiatives for the low-income families in the area. One day, her own house was ransacked by burglars. Then it was burgled again and set alight while she was out. She was so relieved she'd escaped these multiple misfortunes unscathed that she dedicated the site of her razed home as a site for Muslim worship.

The mosque was erected in 1846. Fatimah's great-grandson helped redesign and refurbish the mosque in the thirties. And now, his great-grandson, Abdullah, is leading me through its grounds. He shows me the stone well where they used to draw water for the ablutions. In a nearby garden, 144 of his ancestors point their noses towards Mecca, curved stones for the men, flat-faced grave markers for the women; Abdullah never found out why.

The mosque is currently under the ownership of Majlis Ugama Islam Singapura (MUIS), the Islamic Religious Council of Singapore. But until the late seventies it remained the family's, and Abdullah is still its HR and finance officer. He is also a family trustee and a former board member. Before that, he was an English teacher. But the mosque has always been entwined with his life, providing a vital sense of community. It's like family. For Abdullah, it *is* family. His lineage and the mosque are inextricably linked.

The first Arabs arrived in Singapore around the same time as Sir Stamford Raffles in the early nineteenth century. They were from the Hadhrami families of Yemen, and some of the more prominent names have been immortalized in the Aljunied Roads, Alkaff Crescents, and Alsagoff Buildings that pepper the city. They were an influential community in the nineteenth century, owned large shares of the city's property, and Singapore's position as a base for regional pilgrims on their way to Mecca helped develop its reputation as a hub of Islamic life and the printing of religious texts.

Government rent control and land acquisition in the twentieth century stripped the Arab community of some of this old-school economic influence. There are an estimated 10,000 Arabs[82] in the Lion City but exact numbers are hard to calculate, as there is a growing trend of intermarriage in the modern Arab diaspora. Those returning to visit Hadhramaut have found decades of Southeast Asian influence imported back to the homeland—Javanese batik in Sanaa, sambal belacan chilli paste in Tarim.

Abdullah is one of the only ethnic minorities I've spoken to in Singapore—maybe one of the only ethnic minorities I've even spoken to—who doesn't think race is important. It's partly because his large family—his father was one of eight siblings, and his mother was part of a foster family of twenty-two children—means he never feels like a minority in Chinese-majority Singapore. Partly, it's his own mixed heritage, with a mother of unconfirmed heritage adopted into a Singaporean Arab family after the Second World War. But it's mostly because race will always be a secondary cornerstone to his identity and to his faith. It was what bonded him with the handful of other Muslim pupils at his Anglican school, brought together by the search for halal food or local mosque communities. It provides him with a sense of purpose. Faith is not just skin-deep for Abdullah, it crosses ethnic lines. The mosque conducts sermons in Malay and English, and a large proportion of their visitors are from the Indian community.

Religion is one of the strongest forms of identity. It's one we can be born into or commit ourselves to later in life. It promises a sense of self past death, a continuation in the afterlife. It is invisible to the naked eye but can completely define you. In this way, it's not that dissimilar to the patriotism that ties us to a country and its culture, that inspires us to fight and die for its leaders, to become remembered as a martyr for its people.

Abdullah has been thinking recently about the interplay of religion and politics. Islam's tussle for power after the death of the Prophet. Constantine's decision to slowly integrate Christianity as the main religion of the fourth century Roman Empire. The Nicene Creed, the destruction of pagan sites of worship, the appointment of bishops as trusted political advisors. The baroque extravagance of the Catholic Church in the sixteenth to eighteenth centuries, fighting the Protestant Reformation with gilt and heavenly opulence. Different ideologies and different faiths but always related, tied together by the shared DNA of people and power. The descriptions of the brutal bloodshed in Gaza oversimplified as a 'religious war'. Ancient religious doctrines embroiled in the secular struggles of land ownership and nationhood.

'People have weaknesses,' says Abdullah. 'We have a lot of weaknesses. We're attracted to land ownership, control of oil, wealth. And politics takes advantage of that.'

In a world where religion is a pawn in the dirtiest and bloodiest of conflicts, where at its most extreme, it spreads poison under false promises of glorification and the greater good, how do we know what to believe? How do we, to paraphrase American old-school rock legend Jon Bon Jovi, keep the faith?

Abdullah's answer is simple: slowly. Through tiny kindnesses that you know will never, can never, make up for the magnitude of chaos that's happening on a global scale, but that you do anyway. Through recognizing 'my responsibility, as a Muslim, as an Arab, as a member of the mosque, to make sure that I'm leading by example'.

It's a solid, steady strategy, one that's kept the haphazard architecture of the Hajjah Fatimah Mosque and the memory of its namesake going in the background as Bugis changes and the fiery lights of a hundred arseholes fade into oblivion. It's as solid as Abdullah's conviction. I hope he's right.

EVERYWHERE/NOWHERE

Qingming

It is hot at the cemetery. Hot like a tropical cliché. Hot like a flush of shame. Hot like the furnaces behind us belching crispy warmth or the orchards of joss sticks sending stifling clouds of incense upwards.

Qingming, also known as Brightness Festival or Tomb Sweeping Day, is a day to celebrate the ancestors. You can learn a lot about yourself from those that came before you. There are secrets and tangled roots buried alongside graves.

What I have learned about myself is that I am the sort of person who will spend a scorching afternoon celebrating other people's ancestors as a shameless lion dance troupe groupie.

I love lion dances. I love the way you can be heaved out of sleep by the crashing sound of cymbals or how the air can suddenly throb with the sound of heavy drums, deep and urgent as a foghorn. In a culture prone to reticence, this is our way of shouting celebration from the rooftops. The silky lion sashaying to the movements of the two men operating the costume means a new business has opened, a couple is getting married, or an auspicious occasion has come. There is a lot of celebrating in our neighbourhood; it houses the oldest lion dance troupe in Singapore, the Hok San Association. One thing led to another and here I am, trailing a group of silk-trousered professional giant cat imitators to a graveyard in the name of solid investigative journalism.

Burning is a way to say goodbye. There's something cathartic about the fire's skittish rhythm, the earthy smell of ash as things gently disintegrate. There's a reason why so many love letters go up in flames in the annals of romance. Through the haze, I see stacks of fake bank notes, two-dimensional android phones. I pass a smoking jet-black cardboard Maserati, complete with a pink-faced driver. A pristine sunflower-yellow cutout Babygro curling at the edges.

'It's a way of providing, even in the afterlife,' says Kelvin, a salt-and-pepper-haired Hok San Association member and self-appointed tour guide. 'A very Asian way of saying I love you. I miss you. I hope you have everything you need.'

From Kelvin, I learn that the Peck San Theng cemetery was once the largest in Singapore. Its name means 'pavilions on the jade hills', referring to the twelve buildings scattered across the estate's 324 acres. The area used to be lively with the pageantry of Cantonese death rituals. During the World War II occupation, the Japanese soldiers gave the place a wide berth, fearing ghosts.

Since the area's renovation in the eighties, the place is less spectral and retains just eight acres of its original land.[83] The concrete Columbarium looks a bit like a modern housing block. There are rooms for relatives, urns grouped together as if over an everlasting family meal. There are group rooms for the clans who came over from China generations ago.

The Hok San Clan have come here today to pay their respects. They are here to mourn lives past. But most of all, they are here to boogie.

If you've never seen a lion dance, imagine a cat high on catnip who's just seen his favourite toy dangling just out of reach. Swell this cat to the size of a small elephant and deck it with extravagant tufts of fur trimming, flamboyant face markings, and sometimes, a pair of moveable eyelids with curled eyelashes so fierce they would make any judge on *RuPaul's Drag Race* swoon.

'I was given a pet cat and a ball of string,' recalls lion dancer Chan Yekway. 'For six months, they told me to play with him, watch him, study his moves. Now, when I perform my lion dance, my moves are his. I try to become him.'

There are now around 265 lion dance troupes formally registered in Singapore, catering to a 30 per cent spike in celebratory demand since the pandemic. Some, like Hok San, have traditional Chinese clan associations. Some are commercial ventures. Some are decked with disco beats and LED lights, giving the traditional choreography a modern vibe.

Many are here to compete in a sort of feline musical dance-off punctuated by clashing cymbals and dancing drums. The sounds of a lion dance belong in a cartoon speech bubble. Everything belongs in Badaboom font, in capitals, like in a Roy Lichtenstein painting or a Marvel comic.

BANG! Through the hall of the Daoist God of Prosperity is Tua Pek Kong, whose Sumatra-bound boat washed up accidentally on the Malaysian island of Penang. He decided to stay and became a revered deity.

CRASH! Across the hall of the Three Stars: Fu, Lu, and Shou, cheerful bearded deities of good fortune.

The dance and noise only stop when we reach the Hok San room in the crematorium. The lion has split into two sweaty young men in silk trousers and white T-shirts, joining their fellow clan members in solemn straight lines. How are they still standing? I've lifted the gaping grinning animal head, and there's weight to it. And dancing in this heat is like being slow poached at a disco.

They hold three joss sticks and bow three times—for people, earth, and heaven.

Rows of serious black and white faces stare at us from the front of ceramic urns. For those who left their families behind in China, the clan is a substitute, providing connections and support, linking you together throughout your Singaporean life, and even after it's ended. 'It's so you always have someone to come pay respects,' says Kelvin quietly.

There is a methodical order to the way each urn is labelled. It runs from big to small—province, district, then street—always tracing back to where you came from in China. What a neat way to be defined when you die, your remains tightly packaged in a ceramic pot, marked clearly with your address, so that when strangers are mourning you generations later in a foreign country, there is no doubt over exactly where you came from.

There is an allotted time for contemplation, a chosen segment for silence. It lasts about three minutes. Outside, chaos is calling. There are so many offerings that makeshift trestle tables have spilled out into the courtyard. They buckle under the plates of chicken rice, roasted pork *char siew*, and tiny cups of rice wine. There are refreshments for the living too, small pop-up stalls selling iced cans of chrysanthemum tea that give the space a feel of a village fete or family picnic rather than a festival of the dead.

'It's a way for us to keep the memories of ancestors alive,' explains Kelvin. 'Grandma and Grandpa become less abstract. You can check in with them, eat food together, tell them how things have been going.' He is right. There is nothing lifeless about the gathering in front of us. Casual chat and laughter mix with the smoke. We are here to mourn but also to celebrate. Here to pay respects but also to rejoice at lives well-lived, or lives just lived.

The sound of cymbals and drums pulse through the swollen air as I leave Peck San Theng. You can hear it from the highway back into the city. If you believe in some sort of celestial dimension, chances are it could probably be heard from there too. A message shouted out from those who won't forget you. 'I love you. I miss you. I hope you have everything you need.'

Memories

My grandmother Emily had started to forget. It began with little things. She left food out to rot, chicken braised in soy sauce gravy that turned to marbled jelly and stank. She would blank on events from the week before. Once, she came to visit us in England and strolled confidently into the arrivals hall, clutching someone else's suitcase.

'Ma, this isn't your luggage,' my mum said carefully, as she helped her mother unpack unfamiliar clothes in the spare room.

'Of course it isn't,' my grandma snapped back. 'I would never wear something like that.'

Her husband had passed away a decade ago, a few months short of his sixty-eighth birthday. They'd had a house in the suburbs, with its own garden, but in his final years, my grandfather, Hai Pao, was disillusioned. The sheen of the immigrant's dream had worn thin, the promise of hard work and rootlessness in search of success had fallen short. He hadn't expected to end his life raking his own leaves.

Since his death, my grandmother lived in a small studio apartment downtown where the bedroom was separated by a black wooden concertina screen, inlaid with mother of pearl. It showed the legend of the Daoist Eight Immortals crossing the sea, iridescent animated carvings riding pillowy waves. She had a small dining table in one corner, her qin in another. She used the shared bathroom down the corridor. Simple. Life in one neat, compact box.

My mother bought herself a mobile phone, a black Nokia oblong. Conversations with my grandmother became a long distance rally, garbled back and forth in English and soft fuzzy Shanghainese, which I would struggle desperately to decipher like a secret code. Once, she let the

Nokia exhaust itself. When it buzzed back to life, there were eighteen voicemails waiting.

4.32 p.m.

Alicia ah? Mammy here. Call me.

4.41 p.m.

Alicia. Mammy here. Call me.

4.43 p.m.

Alicia ah?

4.44 p.m.

Alicia?

4.45 p.m.

Alicia. . .??

Vascular dementia, according to the Alzheimer's Association, 'is a decline in thinking skills caused by conditions that block or reduce blood flow to the brain, depriving [brain cells] of oxygen and nutrients'.[84] Connecting matter that passes messages between brain regions becomes sick and shifts, garbling neurological communication like a long-distance phone call in two languages. There isn't any cure, but certain things are said to help. Talking therapy, physical activity or listening to music—the beat helping to untangle jumbled rhythms of thought.

We started visiting Australia more often. There was one place that seemed to calm her, the roaring fountain in the lobby of Melbourne's Crown casino. My mum would drive my grandma there and they would sit side by side on the rim of the pool as above them droplets skydived from the ceiling, flashing like crystals before hitting the bottom in regular splashing beats.

Sometimes, she spoke about Shanghai. Elegant European buildings with arched windows and shop signs in Chinese characters. The crunch of Japanese soldiers' boots on grimy snow. Long term, entombed memories are sometimes said to bubble to the surface in vascular dementia sufferers, pushing more recent events to the sidelines, but according to my mum, my grandma was always like this. She would mention Shanghai often, in an effort to make sure her newly Singaporean children wouldn't forget where they came from. 'I think it was because she missed their homeland. They never really identified as Singaporean and they're roots that were taken away from her,' says my mum. 'She needed to survive.'

For her last years, she moved into a managed residence. It was like she'd become younger. She flirted coyly with my dad, taking her son-in-law's arm as he helped her down the stairs. She made a friend in Pam, a retired Australian fitness teacher, who taught her how to trampoline.

'Higher, Emily, higher!' Pam would shout, and my grandmother would flap her arms, propelling herself towards the ceiling of her tiny room.

The residence phoned my mum. My gran had been smoking smuggled cigarettes in the bathroom; they'd caught her by the smell in her hair. Mum reprimanded her mother like she was a guilty teenager. They rang again two weeks later. She'd been caught again, this time wearing a shower cap to block out the fumes.

I Remember This About You

How much of us is we what we remember?

From the moment we're born, our brains are a bubbling pot of synapses, fusing active connections between neurons like eyes across a house party. Memories form inside us, reactivations of neuron groups whose bonds are particularly strong, but they also form who we are. According to seventeenth century British empiricist John Locke our entire identity is dependent on our memories. In his 1689 'Essay Concerning Human Understanding', Locke asserts that if we're 'losing sight of our past selves . . . doubts are raised whether we are the same thinking thing'. No memories, no me.

When these threads—that not only sew us into the fabric of society but also knit our past selves to our present—unravel, what happens? Does the whole tapestry fall apart, leaving frayed ends that make no sense? Or, despite the holes, is there still some essence of the bigger picture, of something, or someone, that once made sense? Are we reliant on other people's memories of us to shape us?

Here are the things I remember about my grandma Emily. The way she pretended she didn't like her favourite foods so she could sneak them onto our plates. The smell of her dark soy and wine-braised chicken when she cooked it fresh, one of the few recipes she remembered from Shanghai.

And an afternoon in the garden, Australian sun gently warming our suburban Melbourne tiles. A basketball, the same terracotta colour as the tiles, is a streaky orange blur because she's bouncing it so fast. Our mum's mum used to be a semi-professional volleyball player, which, as Lil Sis quips, is ironic, as *our* mum sometimes trips over her own feet.

I can't remember if she was ill already at this point. Some studies say that when people who suffer from dementia start to deteriorate, muscle memory remains. The 'mundane routines' we so easily dismiss are ingrained so deeply in us that they return automatically on days when we struggle to remember where we live. How can these habits not partly form the roots of who we are?

I remember the thud of the basketball hitting the ground like a heartbeat, my grandma's wide, satisfied smile as she taught me to catch and pass. Some things you never forget.

Back Home

London in the summer is hot. Not like Singapore. This is a dry heat, a scathing heat. It's sharp with a dash of British irony. People lounge on the grass lawn outside the Tate Modern, by the elegantly manicured banks of the Serpentine. They spill out of pubs onto pavements like beer bellies over shorts. I am home.

Being back for a month is cramming a year's worth of socializing into a suitcase of limited time. We summarize the past year in a succinct series of anecdotes. We gulp down major life events like shots, buzzing off congratulations and commiserations flowing in quick succession over the course of a meal.

When we move countries there's a part of us that mistakenly believes home is cryogenically frozen until we return. But our friends have grown. Club nights have been usurped by dinner parties. There is a suburban shift; we take commuter trains to Surbiton, St. Albans, past stops with children's book names. There are new people too, small people in corduroy dungarees and lilliputian jeans, who grasp our fingers with sticky hands and side-eye each other suspiciously at the words 'Aunty Mandy'.

Laura is in the same house, a brick terrace off Earl's Court. The front room, which used to host house parties is now a rainbow of plastic bricks, a sloping chunky slide straddles the carpet. Arthur is two, and Douglas is two months old. My childhood friend has become an acrobat. She and her husband are a seamless tag team of juggling children, prams, tricycles, flipping quick jokes and affection into a roulette of household reminders. There's a wholesome lentil salad and dinky home-cooked burgers.

I turn thirty-five. It's a weird age. You've drifted firmly into the territory of 'mid-thirties'. Certain tribunals of the internet sentence you to instant infertility. You could be at a completely different life stage from your best friend. The hangovers last longer and feel like they last forever. But it's also a time that feels surer, stronger, riper with possibilities than before. We're old enough to feel we finally know ourselves and wise enough to know that feeling will probably last all of two minutes.

I walk through the city's guts, away from the gold-tipped Monument, past St. Paul's, once the pinnacle of the city, now stubby in the shadow of skyscrapers. I wind through the crooked streets and jazz bars of Soho, around Russell Square. The British Museum is holding an exhibition on China's Qing dynasty: the last imperial era, the period of the Opium Wars, the Nanking Treaty that ceded Hong Kong to the British. Most of the visitors are Chinese tourists, watching treasures from their homeland through glass cases.

I realize I am split. One foot striding forward, forging stronger friendships and feeling more at home in the Red Dot, while the other clings firmly onto British soil. The two tectonic plates moving further and further apart, risking tearing me in two.

I went to Singapore to learn more about where I come from, but it seems to have done the opposite. On the other hand, it's made me surer about who I am. I will always be the flaky Bad British Asian, my childhood a breadcrumb trail of different schools and gaps in shared cultural references. I will always be the foreigner in Asia, with my ang moh husband and accent that rings of colonial history. Maybe it's in my blood, like my parents and their parents, constantly moving, staking my heart like a flagpole in different countries, belonging everywhere and nowhere all at the same time.

All We Have to Talk About

'But is that all we have to talk about?' asks my friend Isaac, as we walk through rows of black and white photos. 'Is that all we have to say?'

Isaac and I have a lot to say. In fact, in the history of our ten-year friendship, we have very rarely shut up. We met talking at a language course, our tongues hacking clumsily through elementary sentences in Mandarin in a bid to connect to our heritage. We've continued chatting ever since, sadly not in Chinese, but over late post-pub kebabs or the occasional hungover brunch, swapping blog posts, and dreaming up half-baked, high-flying entrepreneurial schemes. But now, in the middle of the British Library's exhibition halls, he is silent, and not just because this is a library with signs throughout the building demanding it.

Chinese and British is an exhibit curated by Dr Lucienne Loh, a Reader in English Literature at Liverpool University and Alex Tickell, the Open University's Global Literatures professor. Maps, manuscripts, and personal artefacts chart over three centuries of Chinese immigration, and 'the lasting impact of Chinese British communities in the UK'. It's the first time I've heard it described that way round with a positive slant—the way we've shaped our surroundings as opposed to the way our new country's have moulded us.

Isaac and I read blurbs about the earliest waves of scholars, merchants, and artisans who travelled to England from China's southern port cities. We learn about the country's first Chinatowns, developed around the communities that settled around the docklands in Liverpool. We're introduced to Asian characters with westernized names: William Macao, the first person in China to settle permanently in Britain, who arrived in the 1770s and lived and worked in Edinburgh for over fifty years. John Anthony, the first Chinese person naturalized as a British citizen through a private act of parliament in 1805.

The exhibition glides to the contemporary. *Parallel*, a short video by filmmaker Rosanna Lee, shows a series of shots from a family dim sum lunch. The jewel-coloured dumplings and the close-up scales of a mottled fish in a tank are brightened just enough to make the mundane seem dream-like. The protagonist is both Chinese and British: mixed-race, unable to understand her Cantonese relatives, even as they share dishes.

The restaurant is in Southend-on-Sea, but it could be any or every dim sum restaurant in the UK. It could be any and every dim sum restaurant in Singapore.

Like the exhibition's title, both Isaac and I are, in our own ways, Chinese and British. While he doesn't speak fluent Mandarin, Isaac can chat with his friends and relatives in perfect Cantonese, having moved to the UK from Hong Kong when he was seven. He studied economics. His side hustle is helping his mother launch her own small business of delicious, perfectly baked mooncakes. In terms of remaining connected to his Asian roots while growing up a continent away, he has always seemed leagues ahead.

So, I'm surprised when, as we shuffle past trading cards of a smiling, bulging-calved Frank Soo, England's first footballer of mixed Chinese heritage, to hear my friend muse that even within the British Chinese community, he felt he never quite fit in. I listen to him talk about the differences between the north London Chinese community where 'the group feels a lot more connected and tight-knit . . . in the southeast there were barely any of us,' the silos, even in the same city, based around local churches, local football teams, favourite K-Pop groups.

We fall under the same diaspora label, as if safety will come in numbers, as if a group can provide some sort of cohesive identity. But sometimes, it can emphasize the differences, differences that we might not even have noticed had we not been cast together, different generations, different countries, different journeys, all shoved in the same boat under one assumed universal experience.

'I feel British. And Chinese. But I don't think I feel British Chinese,' he says. Two sides of himself, plugged in but separate, like pieces from different jigsaws that just happen to fit together. Then, as we're peering into a glass case of mementoes: Dymia Hsiung's *Flowering Exile*, a fictionalized autobiography charting her family's life in Britain from the thirties to the fifties, and a letter from Virginia Woolf to the modernist writer and painter Ling Shuhua:

'Do you think that race is the only thing that Asian writers can write about? Why should that define us? Is that all we have to talk about? Is that all we have to say?' Isaac asks.

Since the eighties, according to the British Library, fiction by writers of east Asian descent based in the UK has flourished. Recently, there have been a small but strong group of non-fiction works. There is Angela Hui's *Takeaway*, and *East Side Voices*, a collection of essays edited by Helena Lee. They explore, even celebrate, the Asian diaspora experience as identity. The 'quiet minority' is becoming louder, seen through our disparate stories, grouped together by our ethnicity.

We are all of course more than our race. We're a patchwork of millions of gigabytes of memories, eras of interests and experiences that have nothing to do with the colour of our skin. Race does not form who we are, it is not always the main plotline of our story. But, if you're an ethnic minority, it will almost always at least have played a supporting role, whether through a throwaway comment of 'apu nehneh', an ostensibly innocuous question of 'Where do you come from?' or the shuffling between different diaspora cliques, wondering if a shared ethnicity is the only thing we have in common. Exhibitions and books and art based on the Asian experience don't have to speak to all of us, or even every part of us. But race can still be a part of our identity without defining who we are, like groups of Chinese arrivals into British cities. A small part with 'lasting impact'.

For now, that is all I have to say.

Gordon

Gordon Chong is what people call a 'character'. He's exuberant, friendly, prone to self-deprecating anecdotes or introductions that veer generously and inaccurately into the lane of hyperbole ('This is Amanda. She's a famous journalist.') He knows everyone at the party. Normally he's the guy who organized the party, especially if it's a gathering of the British Chinese Society, the nonprofit society set up in 2001 as part of the 16,000-strong British Born Chinese Forum to build community among the east Asian diaspora, where Gordon is a member and community organizer.

Gordon came to the UK from Hong Kong in the seventies, when he was seven years old, with his two younger brothers. His father had arrived a few years before and set up a small bakery in London's Chinatown. The family lived in a single room in Holloway, and as his parents didn't speak English, Gordon remembers 'doing all the hard graft translating and helping out with all the bakery work as well'. It's a story shared with a lot of the Asian families in the catering business, he says, except, 'the good thing about bakeries is that you basically only open half a day. The rest of it is just taking care of the place and cleaning, which is pretty easy.'

Years later, one 2020 evening, as he was in a supermarket near his north London home, a man approached him in the drinks aisle and launched at Gordon with a bottle he'd picked up from the shelf.

'All the while he was calling me China Virus,' he remembers. 'As you know that word comes from Donald Trump. This man is not just bad for the Asian diaspora community. He's bad for the world.'

Gordon managed to grab the man's arm before the bottle hit him and left uninjured. He never contacted the supermarket to see if the incident had been recorded on their security cameras or considered reporting it to the police. 'Chinese people are brought up to turn the other way and avoid raising a scene,' he tells me. 'Looking back, it was stupid of me.'

I haven't thought about the pandemic in years. Sometimes, it appears in a cautionary headline or a straight-to-streaming docudrama, then I resurrect it briefly just to push it to the back of my mind, still too slightly recent to relive. I never appreciated how lucky I am to emerge so blithely unscathed.

Gordon's is not an isolated incident. In the first few months of the pandemic, the rate of anti-Chinese hate crimes in the UK nearly tripled.[85] As *Good Morning Britain* host Piers Morgan's causal mockery of 'Ching Chang Chong' Chinese milk drew in over 1,600 Ofcom complaints, across the pond Donald Trump was blithely condemning the 'Chinese virus' and 'Kung Flu'. Congress had to enact a hate crime bill to protect Asians against the swathe of attacks that swelled by 150 per cent in major cities from 2019 to 2020.[86] Between March 2020 and March 2022, more than 11,400 incidences of hate against American Asians were reported across the USA, according to anti-racism group Stop AAPI Hate.[87]

Even recently, new incidents remind us that resentment lingers. Shooting sprees across spas in Atlanta, where six of the eight victims were Asian women.[88] A Lunar New Year's ballroom shooting in Monterey Park.

I've heard a lot about how East Asians, especially the Chinese, are among Britain's 'luckiest minorities'. According to a national census published in 2020, 97 per cent of Britain's Chinese residents continued secondary education to A Level or equivalent, the highest proportion of all the ethnic groups. The Chinese living in Britain are more likely to end up in 'higher managerial, administrative or professional roles' than almost all other ethnic groups and earn a higher household weekly income than almost all other ethnic minorities, second, in both cases, to the Indian community.[89]

There is a small but growing representation of East Asian faces and voices in the mainstream media; mostly pale-skinned, middle-class, internationally accented and educated, of Chinese, Korean, or Japanese heritage; as opposed to the scrappier, less trendy Southeast Asia. The lazy stereotypes of a Chinese cliché are, I have been defensively reassured, overall positive: quiet, hardworking, good at maths.

All this is true. And yet, I wonder how this wave of anti-Asian violence has changed things. How much hate do you have to experience to tackle the model minority myth, to push back against the attitude of some major banks' diversity policies: that we don't count, that we are not a 'real' minority?

Later, a friend of Gordon's and fellow BCS community member tells me about another recent acronym gaining ground in the wake of Covid: BESEA, British East Asian and Southeast Asian. It's apparently gaining popularity as the community wants to stand apart from the better known BAME: Black, Asian, and Minority Ethnic, which lumps all ethnic minorities under the same alphabet gang. It's a way of acknowledging the separate experiences of each minority group, which within themselves will contain many disparate cultures and experiences.

The 'Paki-bashing' sprees that started in the sixties and seventies. The rise in anti-Polish hate crimes post-Brexit. The surge in both anti-Semitic and Islamophobic attacks in London as the conflict in Gaza rages on. Different and disparate minority experiences linked by one commonality: whenever there is a crisis, there is always someone to blame.

In the past few years, Gordon has seen a shift. There's been a rise in anti-Asian hate groups such as CARG (Campaign Against Racism Group), besea.n (Britain's East Asian and South East Asian Network), EVR (End Violence and Racism against East & Southeast Asian Communities), and On Your Side, a helpline and reporting service for East Asian and Southeast Asians experiencing racism and racial hatred.

'There's been an explosion recently,' he observes. 'The older generations, due to their upbringing, they're not that vocal. But the younger generation are a lot more active.'

Since his attack, Gordon has pushed himself to focus his platform towards tackling anti-Asian hate. He's one of the moderators of the Stop Asian Hate Group, another grassroots movement born out of the pandemic. He's spoken in front of parliament and hosted online forums bringing together East and Southeast Asian influencers and content creators, including Filipino-British Ray Roberts and Korean 'halfie' Hanguk Hapa.

'It's not just about the BBC [British Born Chinese] or Chinese,' Gordon says. 'Covid-19 motivated Asians of all communities to unite and do something . . . even I changed my behaviour.'

Sometimes, fear brings out the worst in us. Sometimes, fear brings out the best in us. And sometimes, it just brings us together, clinging in an uncertain huddle against a messy and angry world.

Mile End

While I'm in London, I drop in on my old friend Stamford Raffles.

I got the address from Sean. Sean is Singaporean but moved to London in 2019 to take on a research PhD on networks of empire, family, and art in London's National Gallery, and we met in the gallery café when I profiled him for an art magazine. Over frothy mugs of hot chocolate with clouds of bubbly pink marshmallows, he mentioned that he tracked down Raffles' house for a piece on heritage and empire.

'It's kind of turning history on its head, right? Going to the colonizer's house,' he said with a small shrug, his tiny diamond ear-stud catching the gallery café lights. 'The house was dilapidated. There were two lion statues that were supposed to be at the entrance of the house that had completely toppled over. Which was nice.'

The piece, *Washing White*, includes a two-and-a half-minute video: *Portrait of a Building*. On one half of a split screen, Sean manoeuvres, cat-like, over dust sheet-covered furniture, while in the other half, wide monochrome shots pan over the empty innards of the nineteenth century mansion.

A voiceover, in both English and Mandarin, fires out uneasy statistics. Around 3,375 addresses in the United Kingdom have connections to slave owners, not accounting for those that are linked to colonialism. At least ninety-three National Trust properties have historical ties to the slave trade and colonialism, with fifty linked to the British East India company.

'I was born in a former colony,' it says, 'and felt uneasy being in the house of the colonial master. I was in awe. I was angry. I was upset and intrigued. Then, I felt nothing.'

The voice is Sean's.

It was always in the back of my mind that Raffles was a Londoner, a pupil at a Hammersmith boarding school, then a teenage clerk in the stucco-panelled rooms of the British East India company's Leadenhall Street offices. When he came back to England in the mid-1820s, he was a Barnet boy, living in an elegant estate near Mill Hill, an affluent suburb now known for its private schools and semi-successful football club.

The roads leading up to Burnt Oak station are peppered with neat red brick houses. Braiding salons weave among jerk chicken joints, off-licences, and the modern glass doors of the gospel church. As the bus drives towards Mill Hill, the shopfronts morph into trendy cafés and brasseries.

Highwood House is around a leafy bend from The Rising Sun pub and behind a thick pair of iron security gates. Through the bars, I can see the house is cream-coloured, a pair of svelte Ionic columns standing to attention by the dark wooden door. Neat triangular pediments cap the windows. The lions are not off-duty anymore; they're prim and upright, guarding their territory. On one wall, there is a familiar circular blue plaque, London's own Hollywood star of fame.

Sir Stamford Raffles

Founder of Singapore

Lived here June 1825 to July 1826

There is a Mercedes parked in the driveway. I remember what Sean said to me, his eyes sharp over his cup of chocolatey milk. 'This rich white man who's going to turn this house of a former colonizer into a family home.'

Like a culture or class that remains just out of reach, the gates are closed. What was I expecting? I'm a stranger turning up unannounced on his territory, colonizing a colonizer's home and turning it into my own personal narrative. Threads of the past, twisted by different perspectives, generations of blinkered, biased retellings, all the way to today.

I ring the buzzer and demand the present let me in.

James

James is articulate. James is soft-spoken and polite. James is, despite my preconceptions and the poltergeist of colonial legacy in his home, *nice*.

He was once a Highwood House spectator himself. He grew up in the Mill Hill area and would walk past its iron gates, fascinated by its leafy mystery, its history, its grandeur. Five years ago, by this point a successful property developer with a growing family, he got an unexpected opportunity to view the house with an estate agent. 'That was that,' he says simply. 'We fell in love.'

We don't speak in person. The closest I got to seeing the inside of the expansive former Raffles residence on my visit was a glimpse of ceilings and serene abstract oil paintings, before the housekeeper curtly informed me that the resident of the house wasn't in and shut the door. But I'm persistent. And I'd sat on a bus halfway across London. I left a letter in the mailbox and James, with quintessential British courtesy, had replied by the end of the afternoon. Now, we're speaking over the phone.

The Georgian property had previously been used as accommodation for nursing home staff by former medical director Dr Derek Segall. Later, I find a newspaper article saying that when he first decided to sell the house, Segall was on the lookout for a Singaporean buyer.[90] I'm not sure if this was an attempt at recompense, the colonizer's estate returned to the colonized. I'm also not sure if the idea of living behind the blue circular stamp of Raffles' presence was an uneasy selling point for the Singaporean diaspora in London.

Either way, when James bought it from Segall's daughter nine years later, it was still in the family, divided into four flats for overworked healthcare workers and their families.

The renovations took two years, but James wanted to make sure that the history, character, and grandeur that had first attracted him to the house were protected. He navigated negotiations with the local council, who were initially reluctant to merge housing for four parties into one large family home. He kept the high internal windows, the Georgian panelling. He avoided modern lighting and decor, 'to keep with the style of the house'.

'There are plenty of people who would purchase this property and stick two fingers up to the council,' he reflects. 'Change it. Modernize it. Though it was difficult, I appreciate the need for heritage and to make sure these historical properties are not messed around with.'

My mind is swimming with questions, tangled thoughts, images of carefully preserved properties, and torn down statues. Should we still proudly preserve our heritage when parts of it are so ugly? How do we choose which parts to celebrate, to present to the world like a polished plaque, and which bits to let crumble and rot like debris? And when it comes to the sins of our forefathers, until how many generations should the guilt seep through the bloodline, carrying through, like genes for big feet or freckles?

In the reverent silence of the British Library's airy reading rooms, surrounded by hungover students in hoodies, I find a commemoration by a Conservative MP shortly after Raffles' death: 'It must be remembered that Raffles added Singapore to the British Empire, and, like Warren Hastings, who gave us the Indian Empire, or Cecil Rhodes, the Rhodesian territory, his name must ever be associated with the expansion of British power and influence.'

I wonder how Raffles, who worked to abolish slave ownership in Singapore, would have felt being compared to Rhodes, whose imperial zeal arguably laid the foundations for Apartheid and forced South African diamond miners into conditions close to slavery?

That's the thing about legacy. It blows you up, glorifies your achievements, and grapples with your failings long after you're dust and bones six feet under. And if buildings are bodies, as Sean says they are, then their residents are the organs bringing them to life, linking this building and its future residents forever to your ghosts, whether they like it or not.

'I would say that the only real commonality I have with him is that we are both custodians of a small piece of local history in the form of Highwood House,' James says. And he is, of course, right.

Raffles died in this house on the cusp of forty-five, toppling down the stairs after collapsing from a brain haemorrhage. It's an anti-climactic and somewhat inglorious way to die for a man whose marble avatar still sits in Westminster Abbey and whose residence stands in pristine condition. It's an abrupt full stop to the man who's sparked debates that have long outlived him.

I send Sean a message. 'I spoke with the new owner of Highwood House,' I type. 'He was exactly as you said, a rich white man turning the house of a former colonizer into a family home.'

I don't tell him the rest of it.

My Sister Gets Married in Three Parts

Part 1

We start in Hackney Town Hall. The cool stone lobby is lined with benches, giving the council headquarters the feel of an interview waiting room. Lil Sis and Jon Smith are late, and Dad is early, which means he's spent the last twenty minutes pacing the geometric outlines on the marble floor.

'Sorry, sorry!' they trill in near-married unison. They've been coordinating outfits, right down to matching sunglasses for the photos outside on the steps.

A smiley young woman in spectacles and a blazer takes the couple into a small wood-panelled room. There is an interview, it turns out, a mixture of personal and superficial questions designed as a litmus test of authentic matrimony. Jon Smith panics and almost forgets my mum's name, but they let him off, and the marriage is still allowed to proceed.

We're invited in for the signing. Marriage is a legal process after all, a series of official looking documents signed in the presence of two witnesses. The ink on the paper makes it official. The way Lil Sis takes Jon's hand as they walk down the narrow aisle out the registry office makes it real.

'No more daughters,' mumbles my dad half to himself as we follow them outside. I think he sounds wistful, but maybe that's just wishful thinking. I remind him he's not getting off that easily. Both Lil Sis and I have kept our names.

We pose on the top of the steps, two families photographed in a hodgepodge gaggle of skin tones, hair colours, music tastes, and favourite foods. The confetti from previous weddings scatters across the steps, scraps of leftover happiness.

Part 2

We drive two hours up the motorway to Wonderland. Lewis Carroll used to wander around this estate. He transported his young teenage friend Alice Liddell into the hidden magic in these gardens and made her a hero with his words.

It is a quintessentially English venue for a Chinese tea ceremony. We bulk out my Aunt Zanie's violet Chinese tea set with white ceramic teacups on saucers. The guests mingle too, two races stacked together like mismatched crockery. Lil Sis is wearing a deep red cheongsam. Mum makes a speech introducing the concept of the tea ceremony for the unfamiliar. She makes a joke about *fuks*, and this easily breaks down any cultural barriers.

'Fuk', 福, Cantonese, n. good fortune, or good luck. A million small blessings, a million wishes for your future, handed over in slim red envelopes in exchange for small sips of steaming tea. A hope for a million moments to wake up for, a million small things that say it'll get worse and it'll get better. And throughout it all, I'm happy to be here, alive and with you.

Part 3

The next sun rises over a muddy hill that dips skittishly into a shallow pond. The smooth Italianate face of the building is reflected in jagged outlines in the ripples of a glassy lake.

There are ripples in Lil Sis's dress too. They fan out from her waist in pleats of light white silk. Height is not a dominant genetic trait in the Oon family, but in these eclectic modern rooms, where once Alice clambered through the crowded tunnels of her imagination, my little sister is tall. My little sister is beautiful. My little sister is terrified, washing away a sudden onset of pre-ceremony nerves with deep gluts of Prosecco courtesy of Carroll's old stomping ground.

'You ready?' I ask, threading the back of her dress like I used to tie her laces.

'Ready,' she replies, taking a final swig of bubbles.

Our dad is waiting at the bottom of the stairs. He takes her hand, and for the second time this week, Lil Sis walks down the aisle.

We party. Marriage is a celebration after all, however you choose to celebrate. For Peranakans, the ceremony and its lead-up can last over a week, marked by occasions such as the hair-combing ceremony to mark the couple's transition into adulthood. Eurasian wedding ceremonies take place on a Saturday in a flower-filled church and are followed by feasts of curry puff and sambal sandwiches. They're a melting pot of cultures and traditions and a knotting of family trees. That's why I think we get married in front of our nearest and dearest. It's not just to declare our love. It's to say you have a stake in it too. You're on this journey with us.

At some point Lil Sis ditches the wedding dress for a white halter neck, jeans and, platform sneakers, and she and her new husband mark their first activity as a married couple—blasting out a live performance of The Undertones' 'Teenage Kicks'. Marriage is a double act, knowing each other's beats and chords so deep in your muscle memory that even wrong notes don't matter; you're always in sync. It's just the two of them on the stage. We're not the backing singers. We're not even the groupies. We're in the audience, a messy crowd of happiness, watching, dancing, cheering them on.

Departures

There's a romanticism people have about airports. I blame *Love Actually*, that irrepressible Richard Curtis romantic comedy resurrected every Christmas, showing the gooey happiness of hugs at the arrival gates. They got it right though. There's something about a welcome at the airport. Love standing on the edge of international customs to take you in.

There's less idealism about departures. People don't write odes to the shuffling queues of harried shoeless travellers stacking their electronics into plastic trays for security. But I like departures. Everyone here is in transit. The business traveller in pressed chinos and a blazer hunched over *The Straits Times*. The family piling shrink-wrapped suitcases onto trolleys. The young couple embarking on a new adventure abroad. All of us in limbo on the threshold of something new, rootless, and misplaced.

I don't know Singapore, not really.

It's been four years since we've lived here. At some undefined moment, the Red Dot slipped from being an uncharted tourist territory to home. We stopped scanning for new places to explore and found our favourites. We developed that most prosaic and unadventurous: a routine.

Still, there's an intimacy we'll never be party to. We'll always be outsiders, immigrants in this country of immigrants. It robs us of a certain intimacy but also gives us a unique perspective. Things look different through a foreigner's lens.

Paul and I move through wide, carpeted alleys flanked by duty-free designer boutiques. Glass windows and glassy-eyed people. There's a cheerful souvenir shop selling postcards by the rack. Marina Bay Sands glittering against a stark nighttime backdrop. The Merlion purging crystal clear water into the bay. A compilation of Singapore's greatest hits.

I make my own mental flip book. The apocalyptic beauty of a sunset at Seletar fishing village. The lights of a hundred candles flickering in Hong Lim Park. The thrill of learning a new city, feeling it settle under your skin, soaking in its familiarity, until something reminds you how little you know it. The confused delight of hearing a new Singlish word. The sharp happy surprise of tasting a new dish. The first-date adrenaline flush of making a new friend. Snapshots of what makes a person travel to a country and what makes a person stay.

We are leaving. When we first arrived in Singapore almost four years ago under the gasping sobs of our first tropical rainstorm, we told ourselves it was for a short stint. 'Just a couple of years,' we told ourselves. The self-renewing expat's lie.

Our tickets are return. We are leaving and coming back.

My parents and grandmother are still in Australia. My sister and Jon Smith are still in England, along with Paul's family. And we—our own small unit—somewhere between the two, shuttling and shuffling along airport corridors and becoming further attached to this region that was once a stranger. It's not the most environmentally or even emotionally sustainable dynamic but, for us, for now, it works.

There's no right or perfect way to build a home. Or make a family. No perfect blend of trust, love, comfort, dysfunction, betrayal, or forgiveness that forms the perfect recipe. We're all just muddling along, doing what we can to belong. It's the best we can do. It's all we can do.

People follow the glow of the screens flickering with flight times and gate numbers, deceiving us into thinking that we know exactly where we come from and exactly where we're going.

Author's Note

The word 'foreigner' fascinates me. It's a way of neatly and broadly categorizing anyone who doesn't belong to our country, placing them in the convenient expanse of 'other'. Foreign can be intriguingly exotic or cautiously suspicious, depending on the flavour of the tone and context. Foreigners are defined not by who they are, but who they aren't, which is 'one of us'.

Its synonyms—according to the Collins dictionary—are immigrant, incomer, alien. The vocabulary of sci-fi films or Steven Spielberg Hollywood blockbusters, where a wrinkled pudding-headed, bug-eyed mutant rides tandem bicycles and touches fingertips with a toddler Drew Barrymore.

'E.T. go home.'

It's easy to pine for home when you know where that is. But for our family, transposing our lives in towers of cardboard boxes back and forth from the UK, Australia, Singapore, and Hong Kong, home has always seemed more of an abstract concept, something we'd have to make up as we went along, as opposed to a clearly defined entity defined by bricks, mortar, or national borders.

'Does it feel like home?' my mum would ask, unpacking our familiar furniture into unfamiliar rooms, their floors smelling of disinfectant. I could hear the grasping panic in her voice.

Being rootless can come with setbacks: hostility, loneliness, the feeling of never really fitting in. But it can also be a great gift. It introduces us to new places, people, ways of life, and reminds us of the messy, beautiful vastness of the world. It can make us more comfortable with ourselves, more confident in our differences. It can highlight the underlying commonalities almost all of us share: the need for connection, the desire to belong. It can remind us of the innate generosity of spirit in strangers that extend those things to us with open arms.

Because home is something we can build, and not just with tiles and cement. We can build it through food, through language, memories, through the people we love. Through writing this book, that's what struck me the most. That the things that made people feel most at home were the things they carried around with them, and not in a suitcase.

Afterthoughts

Interview with President Ong Soh Chin, President of AWARE

AWARE is the leading advocacy organization working to end violence against women, including sexual and domestic violence.

How would you summarize being a woman in Singapore today?

In many ways, it's great to be a woman in Singapore. Certainly, I have enjoyed more freedom, opportunities, and rights than my mother did. For that, I am grateful to the pioneers that came before me, including the founders of AWARE.

But gender inequality still persists today, and despite the progress that has been made, there is more to be done.

I am also mindful as a feminist that rights won can also easily be taken back, as can be seen in the reproductive rights struggle in the United States.

Simone de Beauvoir apparently once said, 'Never forget that a political, economical or religious crisis will be enough to cast doubt on women's rights. These rights will never be vested. You'll have to stay vigilant your whole life.' They are powerful words. They are also, sadly, true.

How do you think gender equality in Singapore compares to other Southeast Asian countries? How does Singapore compare on a wider global landscape?

Singapore came in forty-ninth overall in the Global Gender Gap Report 2022[91] by the World Economic Forum and was fourth within the East Asia and Pacific category, behind New Zealand, the Philippines, and Australia. WEF pointed out Singapore's need to close the gender pay gap and encourage more women to join politics, two issues that AWARE has also advocated on.

The most recent UN Convention on the Elimination of All Forms of Discrimination against Women (CEDAW) report,[92] published in 2017, commended the strengthening of laws around harassment, maintenance orders, and human trafficking, but found Singapore to fall short in areas such as: resistance to temporary diversity quotas, lack of comprehensive sexuality education, a persistent gender wage gap, and policies that privileged traditional conceptions of 'family' above others. These are issues that, until today, need progress.

In recent years, we have been pleased to see more concerted efforts made by the Singapore government around advancing gender equality, such as the White Paper on Singapore Women's Development.[93] The White Paper represented the first time that the government had expressly stated a need to make gender equality a fundamental right in Singapore—a landmark moment. We hope to see the scope of these efforts expand in the future, with our principles of inclusion extended to more marginalized sections in our society like single parents, LGBTQ+ people, and domestic workers.

What are the biggest challenges you think face Singaporean women today?

As with many countries, there is a pressing need to distribute the responsibilities of caregiving more equally across genders in Singapore. Despite the strides women have made in the professional environment, on average, women constitute 95 per cent of all persons outside the labour force annually due to family responsibilities. From 2017 to 2021, an average 272,480 women—compared to 13,480 men—were outside the labour force annually due to family responsibilities.

With Singapore set to become a 'super-aged' society by 2026, the question of caregiving for the elderly looms large. Research conducted during the

Covid pandemic paints a bleak picture for the future: despite both spouses working from home, women found themselves doing more domestic labour than pre-pandemic.[94] Women were more likely than their spouses to reduce their working hours or leave their jobs entirely to take on care work. Women with children also find themselves 'sandwiched' between eldercare duties and child-rearing responsibilities.

In the same vein, maternity discrimination is an ongoing problem, as gender role stereotypes around women being caregivers and men being breadwinners remain entrenched. Women with children suffer a 'motherhood penalty'. Statistics from the Ministry of Manpower show that this group has lower labour force participation rates and incomes compared to childless women and men. AWARE's Workplace Harassment and Discrimination Advisory has consistently received a high volume of maternity discrimination cases—85 per cent of the 2022 discrimination cases were reported by pregnant women and mothers. While the recent doubling of paternity leave from two to four weeks indicates changing perspectives on parenthood, and we hope that the Government's introduction of workplace discrimination legislation will create a safer and more equal workplace for mothers, as of now, maternity discrimination is still sadly commonplace.

Violence against women (VAW) is, of course, a major issue facing women and girls in Singapore. VAW occurs in different forms . . . domestic violence (including coercive control) and sexual violence (including technology-facilitated sexual violence and workplace harassment). Technological advancements, and even the growing popularity of artificial intelligence, has spawned new forms of sexual violence, from sexual voyeurism and non-consensual distribution of intimate images to deepfake pornography. Gender-based online harms do not stop at image-based sexual abuse: 40 per cent of Singaporeans have reported seeing misogynistic content in the past two years.[95] AWARE's own research into online misogyny with technology firm Quilt.AI found that accounts run by women on Twitter received twice as many misogynistic comments.[96] As such technology becomes more accessible, we foresee these forms of violence against women to intensify.

What are your main priorities when it comes to the next steps towards gender inequality in Singapore?

As an advocacy group, AWARE has contributed towards and called for strengthening of laws that foster gender equality and conducted public education campaigns on a wide swathe of issues. Our recent efforts have gone towards ensuring that the upcoming anti-discrimination legislation is comprehensive in its coverage. In particular, we have advocated for the inclusion of sexual orientation and gender identity in the list of protected characteristics, as well as the expansion of protections afforded to people with disabilities. Other current research areas include difficulties faced by transnational families (as the majority of migrant spouses in Singapore are women) and improving single parent's access to housing.

Our support services for women in Singapore, which have been running for over thirty years, remain an important pillar of our work. We offer case management, counselling, legal advice, befriending, and other assistance to victim-survivors of gender-based violence. Last year, we received 5,182 calls to our Women's Helpline, and one in four of them pertained to abuse and violence. We also conduct a workshop called Sexual Assault First Responder Training (SAFRT), which has, to date, equipped more than 1,200 members of the public with the skills and knowledge to sensitively support the sexual violence survivors in their lives.

A core part of AWARE's public outreach efforts centre on comprehensive sexuality education (CSE). Our CSE programmes are tailored to suit parents and children and to focus on an area distinctly lacking in the official school curriculum: consent. Stigma around sex prevents parents from talking to their children about consent and other important matters relating to sex and relationships. Our programmes hope to reverse this trend and normalize comprehensive sexuality education at every level of society, so as to nip sexual violence, gender stereotypes, and other unwanted outcomes in the bud.

Mum's Shanghainese Pork Hock Recipe

Ingredients:
A pork hock (ask them to remove the foot)
A generous glug of Chinese wine or mirin
A pinch of five spice powder
A bunch of spring onions with roots cut off, washed and bundled together with a string rock sugar
A glug of dark and/or mushroom soy
A glug of normal soy

Method:

- Wash the raw pork leg.
- Put the leg into a large pot with water. Bring water to boil. Then drain the water and the stuff that comes out of the raw pork when it's been boiling. Don't do it for long. Once it's boiling and the stuff appears, continue for only a few minutes.
- Pour out the water and the stuff. Rinse pork with water.
- Fill the pot with water until it is just covering the pork.
- Put all the ingredients into the pot. Play around with the quantities of both soy sauces to see what works best. You want it dark but not overly so it gets darker with the reduction.
- Bring to a boil.
- Now the hard work starts. Once the water starts to boil, lower heat to low/medium and start bathing the pork with the gravy. Add more dark sauce for colour as you go by.
- Do this for hours until the pork skin is glazed, meat is tender, and gravy has reduced.

Ah Beng Who Cooks' Soy Sauce-glazed Aubergine

Serves one or two people

Ingredients:
Half an aubergine
30 g dark soy sauce
15 g sugar
10 g salt
Water, as needed

Method:

- Dry rub the aubergine and cure it for two hours at least in the chiller to remove excessive water.
- Deep fry the aubergine for four minutes.
- While deep frying, prepare the soy sauce glaze. Mix the dark soy sauce and sugar with the water, simmer it and reduce to a thick consistency.
- Once the aubergine is done, place it face down on the glaze for three mins.
- Drain and serve hot.

Percy's Curry Debal

Ingredients:
1 onion, ½ quartered, ½ thinly sliced
5 tablespoons vegetable oil
3 cm piece of ginger, cut into thinly sliced strips
1 whole chicken (1.5 kg) cut into pieces
4 tablespoons light soy sauce
2 tablespoons pepper
700 ml water
½ cabbage, cut into bite-sized chunks
1 cucumber, peeled, quartered and cut into 5 cm strips
5 tablespoons vinegar
6 to 8 red chilli padi (bird's eye chillies)
200 g bacon bones
1 tablespoon roughly pounded mustard seeds
½ tablespoon salt
2 potatoes, peeled and quartered
10 chicken cocktail sausages

To grind together:
50 g dried chillies
15 shallots
5 large onions
10 cm ginger
10 fresh chillies

Method:

- Take the dried chillies and remove most of the seeds. Cut and soak for 10 minutes. Grind the ingredients together.
- Marinate the chicken in the light soy sauce and pepper for 20 minutes.
- Heat the oil in a pot. Fry thinly-sliced onions and sliced ginger to light brown. Add marinated chicken and bacon bones. Fry until the chicken changes colour. Add the ground ingredients, mustard seeds, salt, and chicken stock.
- Once the ground ingredients are cooked, the oil will rise.
- Add potatoes, cocktail sausages, and water.
- Boil the curry until the potatoes are cooked and the curry thickens, about 10 minutes on medium heat. Add the cabbage, cucumber, and vinegar.
- Remove from the heat and serve hot.
- Garnish with whole chilli padi.

Aunt Elsie's Curry Puffs

Ingredients:

Puff filling (dividing initial dough into 25 pieces; 4.5 kg chicken makes 330 puffs):

½ kg chicken thighs
½ kg chicken thighs (minced)
2 packets curry sauce
6 potatoes (boiled until just cooked then diced)
4 cups finely diced onions
½ teaspoon cumin
2 teaspoons salt
Some curry leaves
Chilli powder to taste

Oil dough:
100 g all-purpose sifted flour
50 g lard or Crisco

Water dough:
25 g all-purpose sifted flour
50 g self-raising sifted flour
170 g shortening
1 tablespoon sugar
¼ teaspoon salt
Water (170 g to 200 g more if required)
2 teaspoons vinegar

Method

Filling:

- Heat oil until hot, then fry onions. When fragrant, add curry leaves and curry sauce, and mix.
- Add cumin, chilli powder, and keep frying on lower flame.
- Add chicken and continue to mix in. Break up minced chicken, otherwise it will clump.
- Turn the flame up so that the chicken will dry out.
- Add salt and continue cooking until the chicken is fully cooked. When chicken is ready, stir in potatoes.

Oil Dough:

- Mix the ingredients together to form a dough.
- Leave in the fridge for at least 1 hour.

Water Dough:

- Add sugar and salt to the sifted flour.
- Rub in the shortening.
- Add water and vinegar to form the dough.
- Leave in the fridge for at least 1 hour.

Making Puff:

- Divide each part of the dough into around 25 pieces. Weigh if required.
- Roll each piece of the water dough into a ball and flatten.
- Wrap the oil dough inside the water dough.
- Flatten each dough piece with rolling pin, roll it like a cigar.
- Turn the dough around and repeat.
- Then cut in half so there are 64 pieces all together.
- Flatten each piece into a cup shape and put in the filling and wrap.
- Deep fry or bake for around ten minutes at 180 degrees Celsius, till golden brown.

Singlish

What happened when I asked Singaporeans their favourite phrase

Gong: like why he so *gong*? Why he so foolish, *lor*?

Lah and *lor*: it's just part of the language. It gives it a local flavour. It's more of a feeling and an emphasis too. The speech is more casual, less formal. If you use *lah* and *lor* it means you're more comfortable with them.

Liao: for when past tense is intended, e.g. I eat *liao* (I have eaten)

Meh: to place a query onto a sentence, e.g. He go there *meh*? (Did he go there?)

Mah: to emphasize the statement just preceding, e.g. he like to eat eggs *mah* (but he likes to eat eggs).

Sia: just something you add to the end of the sentence. Take for example 'I'm so exhausted *sia*.'

Even better, *sian sia*: tired of life.

Sotong: confused. From the Malay for 'squid'. *Blur like sotong* has to be my fave: someone who has their head in the clouds, who is muddle-headed, and generally doesn't have a clue. Conjures such an image with the cloudy squid ink.

Tabao: because I love to eat. *Shiok*. That one is Malay.

Tahan: just *tahan*. Just handle it.

Lepak: it means you just chill. Just slack.

Please, just *give me face can*? Cut me some slack, don't make me look dumb. Basically, help me out!

Wah lau eh!: Literally translates to 'oh my father'. Often used to express surprise or disappointment.

Fil's Thoughts on Back Home

How committed do you think the authorities are to maintaining racial harmony in Singapore?

I think that that is not the right question to ask. The government can try all they want to maintain what they call racial harmony, but the real change happens when people you meet in your everyday life actually care about the issues that minorities face. That is not going to require a top-down solution, but rather a long-term cultural and societal change across all Singaporeans, not just the majority race. It may take decades or even generations.

For example, in the more liberal part of Sydney people of all races were so passionate about campaigning for the yes vote so that Aboriginal and Torres Strait islander people could have more constitutional rights. As a minority Singaporean, it was so heartening to see Australians I knew be so united in this cause and caring about the issues that the minorities were going through. And yet, in Singapore, we are still faced with ignorance and racism from so many majority race Singaporeans. The other day, a neighbour in my cousin's WhatsApp group was warning other members about an Indian man who you couldn't see in the evening because his 'skin is also super dark'. How on earth can the government change this?

If the government does want to create real change and remove the focus on segregation based on race, I reckon it should first start with these:

- Stop collecting race data across all of its government service forms. Why is this even relevant information in the first place? What does stating my race when I am applying for a police check have to do with anything?
- Stop including race on our identity cards and driver's licences. Again, why?

These are just two of many, many examples.

What do you think could be done to tackle Chinese privilege and work towards greater racial harmony in Singapore?

This is a tough question to answer because many, many, many Chinese Singaporeans do not even realize that they are in a position of privilege, and worse, will react very badly if you try to point it out to them. They have internalized the whole 'meritocracy is the path to success' narrative. Sure, hard work will get you places, but what they fail to realize is that they are at a more advanced 'starting point' in life and that their hard work essentially brings much more reward than the hard work of minority Singaporeans. So, meritocracy certainly works for them and not as much for us. I don't think it's too much to ask—just be open to learning about your privilege. I am well aware of my privilege as a middle-class Singaporean: I can speak native English; I have benefited from world-class education, public housing, and transport; I have travelled widely; I have access to healthcare services; I am physically safe when walking on the street—the list goes on. Why can't Chinese Singaporeans also acknowledge that their race adds even more privilege to the list?

Thana

I met Thana when we shared a table at Tekka Centre hawker market. Sometimes short conversations with strangers can share some of the most striking insights about love, life, and loss.

My name is Thana. T-H-A-N-A. I am from India.

No, my parents were from India. I am from here. From Little India.

I've lived here since 1982, a long time already. I married a Singaporean man. No, not Chinese Singaporean. Indian Singaporean. I like it here. The food is good. It is safe.

My husband is no more now. I am alone.

I drive a taxi for Grab, the ride-hailing app. I've done this for four years. When it was the pandemic, it was hard. There was no business, no one wanted to go out. What could we do? Now, things are much better. People are excited. They can do things again.

I didn't move from India. After my studies, I moved to Penang. Penang is wonderful. The food is even better than Singapore! I was happy there.

But, one day, I visited Singapore to see my brother. He was living there; he's moved back to Malaysia now. I went out with him. I met his friends. Later, my brother called me.

'My friend has fallen in love with you,' he said.

I had met him once.

We got married in Singapore. My parents are from quite a traditional family, and they believe that once you're married you should move to the husband's house. So I gave up my Malaysian passport, and we moved here.

He was a nice man. A very kind man. God loved him so much. That's why he took him early.

I still find ways to be happy. The Singaporean passport is better than a Malaysian one. And it is safer here than in Penang. In Penang, you cannot drive around alone, not unless you know the roads very, very well. Here, I can drive, even in the middle of the night and know I am safe.

I love to drive. Before I got this job, I was working in customer service for Singapore General Hospital. Customer service is hard. And in a hospital, you deal with people at their very worst.

I was in the middle of getting my driving licence and every lesson was like a breath of fresh air. My friend said, 'You love to drive. Why don't you apply to do this?' So I applied to Grab. I didn't think I'd get it. I had to do this test; it was really difficult! But I passed, and now I am so happy.

I love getting to know customers. Sometimes, people don't want to talk. That's okay; then I don't talk, too. I respect that. Sometimes, they tell me all their secrets.

I had one man in my car once; he used to be in the police force. Then, he became a private bodyguard. He said his new colleagues were always picking on him, always trying to make him look bad in front of the boss. It got so bad, he wanted to quit. I remember him telling me this, so upset. He has two small children, girls, how to quit?

I told him, 'Have trust in what's inside. What's inside you. It doesn't matter what comes from outside. Everyone will always have something to say, but if you know inside that you are hardworking, that you are doing your best. That's enough.'

What do I like to do? I like to drive. After this, I will drive some more. Then, I will go home, cook dinner, listen to music, then go on Facebook until I fall asleep. I like to be busy. Too much time alone and I find . . . too much space for thoughts. I don't like to let them run inside my head.

Acknowledgements

There are so many people who helped make this book possible.

Thank you to Nora for believing in the story and for your guidance throughout the process; and to Amberdawn, Divya, Sneha, and the rest of the team at Penguin SEA for your thoughtful and sharp editing.

Thank you to the National Library and the National Archives of Singapore and the British Library in London for being such a valuable and important wealth of research, whatever the subject. And for being happy refuges for writing, people-watching, provider of refreshments, and havens of air-conditioning/heating against the respective Singaporean/British weather.

Thank you to Victor Yue of the Singapore Heritage Society. Even though your name doesn't appear in these pages, you have been a tireless and patient provider of advice, stories, and information in the background. You've introduced me to a fair few of the places that appear in these chapters and have always been at the end of a text to answer my constant questions on Singapore heritage.

Thank you to the NGOs—Project X and TWC2—and the activists—Kokila Annamalai and Kirsten Han—for the work you do and for letting me reference it here.

Thank you to the experts and academics, Professor Kwa Chong Guan, Dr Ritu Jain, Assistant Professor Luke Lu, Amy Zhao, Sabrina Ooi, who shared their insights and expertise.

Thank you to the artists, Sean Cham, Rosanna Lee, Yip Yew Chong, for their nostalgic, beautiful, and brave work exploring themes of heritage, colonialism, nationhood, and identity split across different cultures. And for letting me share and reference that work here.

Thank you to the people who have let me share their lives and stories. Chua Mui Hoong, Loretta, Abdullah, Percy, Jason, Alvin, Yinzhou, Helen, Lina and Nassib, A.K.M. Mohsin, K. Kamalanathan, Hassan, Hossain, Mohammad Bin Poh, Thana. Your generosity of spirit and time, and the honesty and humour with which you opened up taught me so much, not just about Singapore but also about the warmth of its people.

Thank you to Gordon Chong for sharing your story and introducing me into the British Chinese community in your brilliantly unique way.

Thank you to James for replying to a random handwritten note by a stranger and opening up so generously about your home and its history.

Thank you to Venky, Lauren, Mel, Laura, Filzah, Laura, Isaac, Charlotte, Bryony, Rosanna, Anna. They say your friends are your chosen family, and I feel extremely lucky to have found the best chosen families on both continents.

To Uncle John, thank you for sharing your passion for our family history; for your research; and for your constant dedication to documenting our moments as an extended family, whether through old keepsakes or your ubiquitous selfie stick.

Thanks to Auntie Elsie, Auntie Zanie, and my cousins, for always being family, even when we are on opposite sides of the world.

Thanks to my grandparents. You are the reason this book exists and where it all started.

Thank you to Mum, Dad, and Lil Sis, for the practical stuff: patiently sharing and repeating family history, digging up old photos and memories, and proofreading first drafts; and the not-so-practical stuff: for making a home whatever country we're in, for the years of love, support, laughter, and just enough dysfunction to make a good story. Thank you, newest family member, Jon Smith, for embracing being part of the madness.

To Paul, thanks for believing in me and this story. Thanks for your support, encouragement, and accompanying me up a mountain and to various corners of Singapore. Thanks for being my fellow adventurer, my best friend, and the love of my life. Home is where you are.

Notes

1 Justin Ong, 'Race-based Data in Population Census Needed for S'pore to Help Ethnic Groups Meaningfully: Indranee,' The Straits Times, June 17, 2021, https://www.straitstimes.com/singapore/politics/race-based-data-in-population-census-needed-for-spore-to-help-ethnic-groups.

2 Singapore Department of Statistics. 'Singapore Population Statistics 2010-2020,' 2021. https://www.singstat.gov.sg/-/media/files/publications/cop2020/sr1/findings.pdf.

3 Yusof Sulaiman, '2020 Census – a Community Perspective,' The Karyawan, January 14, 2022, https://karyawan.sg/2020-census-a-community-perspective/.

4 Goh Yan Han and Grace Ho, 'Tharman believes S'pore is ready for a non-Chinese PM,' The Straits Times, 15 November 2024, https://www.straitstimes.com/singapore/politics/tharman-believes-s-pore-is-ready-for-a-non-chinese-pm.

5 'Rapper Subhas Nair to be charged over comments on race and religion, breaching terms of conditional warning,' CNA, 28 Oct 2021, https://www.channelnewsasia.com/singapore/rapper-subhas-nair-be-charged-over-comments-race-and-religion-breaching-terms-conditional-warning-2275791.

6 Koh Ewe, 'A Singaporean Rapper Tried to Call Out Racism. He's Been Sentenced to Jail For His Statements,' Time, 5 September 2023, https://time.com/6310667/subhas-nair-singapore-racism-rapper-jail-sentence/.

7 Koh Ewe, 'A Singaporean Rapper Tried to Call Out Racism. He's Been Sentenced to Jail For His Statements,' Time, September 5, 2023, https://time.com/6310667/subhas-nair-singapore-racism-rapper-jail-sentence/.

8 Admin, 'Why Was There No Singapore Before Raffles? - ISEAS-Yusof Ishak Institute,' ISEAS-Yusof Ishak Institute, March 21, 2020, https://www.iseas.edu.sg/media/event-highlights/special-lecture-series-why-was-there-no-singapore-before-raffles/.

9 'Thomas Stamford Raffles: Schemer or Reformer?', Syed Hussein Alatas, 2020

10 Sun, Rebecca, 'Constance Wu Explains "Fresh Off the Boat" Renewal Outburst: "I Had to Give Up Another Project",' The Hollywood Reporter, 10 May 2019, https://www.hollywoodreporter.com/tv/tv-news/constance-wu-tweets-fresh-boat-renewal-dislike-1209752/.

11 Kim, Juliana, 'Constance Wu's reveal speaks to the profound pressure Asian American women face,' NPR, 18 July 2022, https://www.npr.org/2022/07/18/1112055817/constance-wu-asian-american-women.

12 'Crazy Rich Asians 2 unlikely, admits director Jon M Chu,' CNA, November 15, 2024, https://cnalifestyle.channelnewsasia.com/entertainment/crazy-rich-asians-2-unlikely-says-director-413776.

13 Mukunthan, Michael, 'Loke Wan Tho,' National Library Board, n.d., https://www.nlb.gov.sg/main/article-detail?cmsuuid=0aa25928-d7b2-4c71-a0a1-3dffe99cadff.

14 Staff Writer, 'Singapore Touts Top Share of Women CEOs, Pushes for More,' Nikkei Asia, May 11, 2022, https://asia.nikkei.com/Business/Business-trends/Singapore-touts-top-share-of-women-CEOs-pushes-for-more.

15 'Global Gender Gap Report 2023,' World Economic Forum, n.d., https://www.weforum.org/publications/global-gender-gap-report-2023/in-full/benchmarking-gender-gaps-2023/; 'SCWO highlights Singapore's gender equality progress,' Gov Media, n.d., https://govmedia.com/videos/scwo-highlights-singapores-gender-equality-progress; 'Singapore's Global Gender Gap score from 2014 to 2023,' Statista, n.d., https://www.statista.com/statistics/972905/global-gender-gap-score-singapore/.

16 @aiasingapore, 'As we celebrate #InternationalWomensDay this month, let's recognise the incredible contributions that women make to society.' Instagram video, March 26, 2023, https://www.instagram.com/p/CqPVgN0umuU/.

17 'The Rise and Fall of Confucian Family Values,' Institute for Family Studies, n.d., https://ifstudies.org/blog/the-rise-and-fall-of-confucian-family-values.

18 CNA, 'Masagos Zulkifli on Baby Bonus for Single Unwed Parents,' CNA, April 5, 2023, https://www.channelnewsasia.com/watch/masagos-zulkifli-baby-bonus-single-unwed-parents-3327281.

19 Theresa Tan, 'Govt's Support for Family Extends to Unwed Parents and Their Children: Sun Xueling,' The Straits Times, April 1, 2022, https://www.straitstimes.com/singapore/community/govts-support-for-family-extends-to-unwed-parents-and-their-children-sun-xueling.

20 Shailey Hingorani, 'The Road to Housing for Single, Unwed Mothers Is Clearer but Still Bumpy,' AWARE, March 8, 2020, https://www.aware.org.sg/2020/03/the-road-to-housing-for-single-unwed-mothers-is-clearer-but-still-bumpy/.

21 'Approach to Support Single Unwed Parents in their Caregiving Responsibilities,' Ministry of Social and Family Development, July 5, 2021, https://www.msf.gov.sg/media-room/article/Approach-to-Support-Single-Unwed-Parents-in-their-Caregiving-Responsibilities.

22 'This Is Home: 177 new S'poreans Take the Pledge at Annual Citizenship Ceremony,' The Straits Times, Augut 18, 2024.

23 'In Our Time,' CNA, January 1, 2020, https://www.channelnewsasia.com/watch/our-time/sixties-singapore-boleh-1484881; '1965: The Gender Gap at a Glance,' Singapore Women's Hall of Fame, n.d., https://www.swhf.sg/tlow-2-panel-1/.

24 National Archives, 'Prime Minister's Speech at the 5th Anniversary Celebration of the Yio Chu Kang Community Centre on the 18th December, 1965.'

25 CNA, 'Should women do National Service now? Societal cost will 'far outweigh' benefits, says Ng Eng Hen,' CNA, May 9, 2022

26 Syarafana Shafeeq, `Number of Suicides in Singapore drops in 2023, Lowest since 2000,' The Straits Times, July 12, 2024, https://www.straitstimes.com/singapore/number-of-suicides-in-singapore-drops-in-2023-lowest-since-2000.

27 Remember Singapore, 'Gongs, Long Hair and Chewing Gums,' June 19, 2014, https://remembersingapore.org/2014/06/19/gongs-long-hair-chewing-gums/; Seow, Peck Ngiam, 'Anti-yellow culture campaign,' National Library Board, September 2021, https://www.nlb.gov.sg/main/article-detail?cmsuuid=8e493ee4-1832-4fec-96ee-a0a6b3efab87.

28 National Gallery, Violet Oon, conversation with Tamares Goh, February 29, 2020.

29 '"Is It Because I'm Chinese?": Chinese Privilege in Singapore,' Aaron K. Ho, Independently published, 2021

30 Mokhtar, Faris, 'Survey points to social class divide among Singaporeans,' Lee Kuan Yew School of Public Policy, 28 December 2017, https://lkyspp.nus.edu.sg/docs/default-source/ips/today_survey-points-to-social-class-divide-among-singaporeans_28122017.pdf?sfvrsn=1553710a_2.

31 Yeo, Nikki, 'Survey Points to Social Class Divide Among Singaporeans,' Today, June 5, 2024, https://www.todayonline.com/singapore/survey-points-social-class-divide-among-singaporeans.

32 CNA, 'Is Singapore Still Based on Equality? | Regardless of Class | Full Episode,' October 15, 2019, https://www.youtube.com/watch?v=_pDdd16XtIY.

33 'Destitute Persons Act 1989: 2020 REVISED EDITION,' Singapore Statutes Online, 1 December 2021, https://sso.agc.gov.sg/Act/DPA1989.

34 'Homeless in Singapore - A Nationwide Street Count,' Lee Kuan Yew School of Public Policy, n.d, https://lkyspp.nus.edu.sg/research/social-inclusion-project/homelessness-street-count/key-findings.

35 Ng, K. H., & Sekhon Atac, J. S. (2022). 'Seeking Shelter: Homeless during the COVID-19 Pandemic in Singapore.' Singapore: Lee Kuan Yew School of Public Policy. https://lkyspp.nus.edu.sg/research/social-inclusion-project/homelessness-street-count/key-findings.

36 Stolarchuk, Jewel, 'The Face of the Government's Hawker Policies, Amy Khor, Reveals She Is the Daughter of a Hawker,' The Independent Singapore, October 30, 2018, https://theindependent.sg/the-face-of-the-governments-hawker-policies-amy-khor-reveals-she-is-the-daughter-of-a-hawker/.

37 Deborah Lau, 'Singapore Students with Depression, Anxiety Symptoms Miss 24 Days of School Yearly on Average: Study,' CNA, May 19, 2023, https://www.channelnewsasia.com/students-anxiety-depression-lose-average-24-days-year-school-4632256#:~:text=The%20study%20found%20that%20depression,of%20school%2C%20the%20survey%20found.

38 'Is Singapore's Unemployment Rate in a 'Goldilocks' State?,' *The Business Times*, October 24, 2023, https://www.businesstimes.com.sg/singapore/singapores-unemployment-rate-goldilocks-state. rate-goldilocks-state

39 'Unemployment Rates Around the World 2024,' Global Finance, April 18, 2024, https://gfmag.com/data/economic-data/world-unemployment-rates/.

40 National Archives of Singapore, Summary of Speech by the Prime Minister at the Official Opening of the Premises of the Jurong Town Residents' Association on 31 July, 1970.

41 'Singapore Tops Ranking of World's Best Places to Be Amid Covid-19 Pandemic,' The Straits Times, April 27, 2021, https://www.straitstimes.com/asia/the-best-and-worst-places-to-be-in-the-world-as-covid-19-variants-outrace-vaccinations.

42 Heijmans, Philip, 'Singapore keeps dorm migrants segregated even as pandemic abates,' The Japan Times, 20 April 2021, https://www.japantimes.co.jp/news/2021/04/20/asia-pacific/singapore-migrant-dorms/.

43 John Geddie and Aradhana Aravindan, 'Spate of suicides among migrant workers in Singapore raises concern,' Reuters, August 6, 2020.

44 Song Yihang, 'Shedding Light on the Plight and Laws Regulating Migrant Worker Dormitories in Singapore,' National University of Singapore, Law, https://law.nus.edu.sg/impact/covid-19-shedding-light-on-the-plight-and-laws-regulating-migrant-worker-dormitories-in-singapore/.

45 Kok Yufeng, 'Larger living spaces, better ventilation among improved standards for new migrant worker dorms,' The Straits Times, September 17, 2021, https://www.straitstimes.com/singapore/improved-standards-for-new-migrant-worker-dormitories.

46 'Migrant workers suffer in Singapore's hidden lockdown,' Financial Times, June 6 2022, https://www.ft.com/content/4c63dea0-9ebd-4170-b978-5dce0c5e7f99.

47 Koh, Sarah, 'Construction worker dies after being struck by falling steel frame at Pioneer worksite, breaching terms of conditional warning,' The Straits Times, 18 August 2024, https://www.straitstimes.com/singapore/construction-worker-dies-after-being-struck-by-falling-steel-frame-at-pioneer-worksite; Kok Yufeng, 'Construction worker dies three days after iron pipe fell five storeys and struck him,' The Straits Times, 10 August 2024, https://www.straitstimes.com/singapore/construction-worker-dies-after-iron-pipe-fell-five-storeys-and-struck-him; Lim, Kolette, 'Worker dies in accident at Sentosa worksite,' The Straits Times, 29 September 2024, https://www.straitstimes.com/singapore/man-dies-in-work-related-accident-at-sentosa.

48 'Work Permit for Foreign Domestic Workers - FDW Work Permit Singapore,' VisaGuide.World, October 25, 2022. https://visaguide.world/asia/singapore-visa/work-passes-and-permits/foreign-domestic-workers/#google_vignette.

49 'Over 60pc Bangladeshis lost jobs to Covid in March-April 2020: Survey,' The Financial Express, May 6, 2021, https://thefinancialexpress.com.bd/economy/bangladesh/over-60pc-bangladeshis-lost-jobs-to-covid-in-march-april-2020-survey-1620272075.

50 Md Rezaul Karim, 'Data Quality in the World Bank's Bilateral Remittance Report: Case Study of Bangladesh and India,' Finextra, 25 November 2024, https://www.finextra.com/blogposting/27276/data-quality-in-the-world-banks-bilateral-remittance-report-case-study-of-bangladesh-and-india#:~:text=According%20to%20estimates%20by%20the,across%20Europe%20and%20other%20regions.

51 Diman, Hairianto, 'The Big Story: Food meant for migrant workers left unattended outside dormitories; MOM investigating,' The Straits Times, 10 April 2023, https://www.straitstimes.com/multimedia/the-big-story-food-meant-for-migrant-workers-left-unattended-outside-dormitories-mom-investigating.

52 Sim, Cheryl, 'Little India riot,' National Library Board Singapore, n.d., https://www.nlb.gov.sg/main/article-detail?cmsuuid=1665605a-de43-4e02-a8aa-c3d8f42a1c8c.

53 'Racial Riots (1964 and 1969),' SG101, n.d., https://www.sg101.gov.sg/social-national-identity/examples/racialriots/.

54 Stolarchuk, Jewel, 'Yet another migrant worker passes away in construction site accident,' The Independent Singapore, October 24, 2024, https://theindependent.sg/yet-another-migrant-worker-passes-away-in-construction-site-accident/; Kok Yufeng, 'Two workers killed in accident at North-South Corridor worksite in Lentor Avenue,' The Straits Times, September 18, 2024 https://www.straitstimes.com/singapore/two-workers-killed-in-accident-at-north-south-corridor-worksite-in-lentor-avenue.

55 Wong, Andrew, 'Up to 30 years' jail for possession of drugs including cannabis with roll-out of stricter drug laws from June,' The Straits Times, June 2, 2023, https://www.straitstimes.com/singapore/up-to-30-years-jail-for-possession-of-cannabis-with-roll-out-of-stricter-drug-laws-from-june.

56 Hamzah, Aqil, 'Three arrested and $131k of drugs seized in drug busts in Telok Blangah, Geylang,' The Straits Times, Jun 20, 2024, https://www.straitstimes.com/singapore/three-arrested-and-131k-of-drugs-seized-in-drug-busts-in-telok-blangah-geylang; 'Cough syrup made in "unsanitary" Geylang condo seized in crackdown on illegal medicine,' CNA, May 20, 2024, https://www.channelnewsasia.com/singapore/cough-syrup-made-unsanitary-geylang-condo-unit-illegal-medicine-hsa-police-4349166.

57 'Marina Bay Sands Hires Law Firm to Probe Over $1.36 Billion in Money Transfers,' *The Straits Times*, September 17, 2020, https://www.straitstimes.com/business/companies-markets/marina-bay-sands-hires-law-firm-to-probe-us1-billion-in-money-transfers.

58 Chanyaporn Chanjaroen, 'Singapore Sands Sued by Chinese Ex-Client Claiming $6.6 Million,' Bloomberg, October 10, 2019, https://www.bloomberg.com/news/articles/2019-10-10/singapore-sands-sued-by-chinese-ex-client-claiming-6-6-million.

59 'Laws on Procuring Sex Workers & Sexual Services in Singapore,' Singapore Legal Advice, n.d., https://singaporelegaladvice.com/law-articles/laws-procuring-sex-workers-sexual-services-singapore/.

60 'Maintaining Public Order,' Ministry of Home Affairs, n.d., https://www.mha.gov.sg/what-we-do/maintaining-law-and-order/maintaining-public-order; 'Public Assemblies and Processions in Singapore,' Singapore Legal Advice, 6 May 2022, https://singaporelegaladvice.com/law-articles/public-assemblies-and-processions-in-singapore-police-permits-and-the-public-order-act/.

61 Regan, Helen, 'Campaigners make last effort to save man with intellectual disabilities from execution in Singapore,' CNN, 9 November 2021, https://edition.cnn.com/2021/11/08/asia/singapore-nagaenthran-dharmalingam-death-penalty-intl-hnk/index.html; 'Singapore urged to halt double execution planned for Wednesday,' Al Jazeera, 15 February 2022, https://www.aljazeera.com/news/2022/2/15/

amnesty-appeals-for-singapore-to-halt-executions#:~:text=Nagaenthran's%20appeal%20has%20been%20postponed,to%20death%20a%20year%20later; Tan, Yvette, 'Singapore executes man on drugs charge, rejecting mental disability plea,' BBC, 27 April 2022, https://www.bbc.com/news/world-asia-61239221.

62 'Singapore Announces Plans to Execute More Death-Sentenced Prisoners Convicted of Non-Violent Drug Offenses,' Death Penalty Information Center, 14 August 2023, https://deathpenaltyinfo.org/singapore-announces-plans-to-execute-more-death-sentenced-prisoners-convicted-of-non-violent-drug-offenses.

63 Han, Kirsten, 'Aren't we supposed to be all about rule of law and due process?,' We, the Citizens, 22 April 2023, https://www.wethecitizens.net/arent-we-supposed-to-be-all-about-rule-of-law-and-due-process/.

64 'Singapore executes Tamil man despite international outcry,' Tamil Guardian, 26 April 2023, https://www.tamilguardian.com/content/singapore-executes-tamil-man-despite-international-outcry.

65 Ratcliffe, Rebecca, 'Singaporean on death row denied access to lawyers, say activists,' The Guardian, 24 April 2023, https://www.theguardian.com/world/2023/apr/24/singaporean-on-death-row-denied-access-to-lawyers-say-activists-tangaraju-suppiah.

66 'Corrections regarding false statements of fact concerning the capital sentence that was meted out to Tangaraju S/O Suppiah,' gov.sg, 19 May 2023, https://www.gov.sg/article/factually190523.

67 '"Right to Remain Silent" to Singapore Police: Does It Exist?,' Singapore Legal Advice, 25 October 2024, https://singaporelegaladvice.com/law-articles/right-to-remain-silent-police-singapore/.

68 'More Singapore Residents Support the Use of the Death Penalty,' Ministry of Home Affairs, n.d., https://www.mha.gov.sg/mediaroom/press-releases/more-singapore-residents-support-the-use-of-the-death-penalty/.

69 'Singapore Announces Plans to Execute More Death-Sentenced Prisoners Convicted of Non-Violent Drug Offenses,' Death Penalty Information Center, 14 August 2023, https://deathpenaltyinfo.org/singapore-announces-plans-to-execute-more-death-sentenced-prisoners-convicted-of-non-violent-drug-offenses.

70 'Our Story,' Changi Airport Group, n.d., https://www.changiairport.com/en/corporate/about-us/the-changi-airport-story/our-story.html.

71 Khalid, Cam, 'Kampung Life: The last villages in Singapore and the stories behind them,' Time Out, 5 February 2022, https://www.timeout.com/singapore/things-to-do/kampung-life-the-last-villages-in-singapore-and-the-stories-behind-them.

72 Koh Wan Ting, 'Otter family that established home in Seletar estate transferred out after earlier reports of intrusion,' CNA, 17 October 2022, https://www.channelnewsasia.com/singapore/otter-family-seletar-kill-fish-transfer-residential-estate-nparks-monitor-3011076.

73 Neo Chai Chin, 'Singapore's prison without walls made the world sit up in 1960s. How did it fall apart?,' CNA, 28 January 2023, https://www.channelnewsasia.com/cna-insider/singapore-prison-without-walls-1960s-riot-island-pulau-senang-3235821.

74 Ibid.

75 Ibid.

76 'Pulau Senang,' National Library Board, n.d., https://www.nlb.gov.sg/main/article-detail?cmsuuid=42b6bfb3-5af0-4589-ad46-c6f92502272a#:~:text=The%20Pulau%20Senang%20settlement%20closed,Ministry%20of%20Interior%20and%20Defence.

77 Clarke, Chris, 'Do opposites really attract? Here's how UQ research concluded otherwise,' The University of Queensland, June 13, 2024, https://www.uq.edu.au/research/article/2024/06/do-opposites-really-attract-heres-how-uq-research-concluded-otherwise.

78 Olivia Miwil, 'Kinabalu Park Expects More Tourists This Year,' NST Online, January 16, 2022, https://www.nst.com.my/news/nation/2022/01/763420/kinabalu-park-expects-more-tourists-year.

79 Liu, Shuang, Maher, Jessica, Sheer, Vivian C., 'Through the Eyes of Older Chinese Immigrants: Identity, Belonging and Home in a Foreign Land,' The University of Queensland, Australia, n.d., https://tinyurl.com/2tyhy5k8.

80 Doniger, Wendy, 'Kali,' Britannica, October 22, 2024, https://www.britannica.com/topic/Kali.

81 Meiyu, Lee, 'Bugis Street: From Sleazy to Sanitised,' Biblioasia, October 1, 2015, https://biblioasia.nlb.gov.sg/vol-11/issue-3/oct-dec-2015/bugis/; 'Bugis Street,' National Library Board, n.d., https://www.nlb.gov.sg/main/article-detail?cmsuuid=e3a4d2cb-1120-4b83-bbc4-a0874b0f232f#:~:text=Bugis%20street%20possibly%20got%20its,various%20parts%20of%20Southeast%20Asia.

82 Vittoria Volgare Detaille, 'Singapore's Arab Street: A Closer Look at the Community Building a New Legacy,' Middle East Eye, n.d., https://www.middleeasteye.net/discover/singapore-arab-street-building-new-legacy#:~:text=The%20Alkaff%20family%20was%20responsible,between%208%2C000%20to%2010%2C000%20people.

83 Lee Kok Leong, 'Kwong Wai Siew Peck San Theng: The cemetery built by the Cantonese in Singapore,' Culturepaedia Singapore, n.d., https://culturepaedia.singaporeccc.org.sg/communities/dialect-group/kwong-wai-siew-peck-san-theng-the-cemetery-built-by-the-cantonese-in-singapore/.

84 'Vascular Dementia', Alzheimer's Disease and Dementia, n.d., https://www.alz.org/alzheimers-dementia/what-is-dementia/types-of-dementia/vascular-dementia#:~:text=Vascular%20dementia%20is%20a%20decline,them%20of%20oxygen%20and%20nutrients.

85 Mercer, David, 'Coronavirus: Hate crimes against Chinese people soar in UK during COVID-19 crisis,' Sky News, May 5, 2020, https://news.sky.com/story/coronavirus-hate-crimes-against-chinese-people-soar-in-uk-during-covid-19-crisis-11979388.

86 NBC News, 'Anti-Asian hate crimes increased by nearly 150% in 2020, mostly in N.Y. and L.A., new report says,' https://www.nbcnews.com/news/asian-america/anti-asian-hate-crimes-increased-nearly-150-2020-mostly-n-n1260264

87 Edwin Rios, 'Hate Incidents Against Asian Americans Continue to Surge, Study Finds,' The Guardian, December 15, 2022, https://www.theguardian.com/us-news/2022/jul/21/asian-americans-hate-incidents-study.

88 McDonnell, Giulia, del Rio, Nieto, and Sandoval, Edgar, 'Women of Asian Descent Were 6 of the 8 Victims in Atlanta Shootings,' The New York Times, 17 March 2021, https://www.nytimes.com/2021/03/17/us/asian-women-victims-atlanta-shootings.html.

89 'Chinese Ethnic Group: Facts and Figures,' Ethnicity Facts and Figures, January 27, 2020, https://www.ethnicity-facts-figures.service.gov.uk/summaries/chinese-ethnic-group/.

90 '£3.5m for home of Singapore founder Raffles,' The Standard, 13 April 2012, https://www.standard.co.uk/hp/front/ps3-5m-for-home-of-singapore-founder-raffles-6628173.html.

91 'Global Gender Gap Report 2022,' World Economic Forum, September 10, 2024, https://www.weforum.org/publications/global-gender-gap-report-2022/.

92 'CEDAW/C/SGP/CO/5: Concluding observations on the fifth periodic report of Singapore', *United Nations*, November 21, 2017, https://www.ohchr.org/en/documents/concluding-observations/cedawcsgpco5-concluding-observations-fifth-periodic-report

93 'Singapore Womens Development White Paper,' n.d., https://www.reach.gov.sg/Participate/conversations-on-singapore-womens-development.

94 'Singapore women are doing more unpaid domestic & care work than the men think they are,' Ipsos, May 7, 2021, https://www.ipsos.com/en-sg/singapore-women-are-doing-more-unpaid-domestic-care-work-men-think-they-are.

95 'Singaporeans' Attitudes Towards Gender Equality, Feminism and Online Behaviour,' Ipsos, March 9, 2022, https://www.ipsos.com/en-sg/singaporeans-attitudes-towards-gender-equality-feminism-and-online-behaviour.

96 AWARE Media, 'Online Misogyny Manifests in Resentment Around National Service and Misconceptions Around Gender-based Violence, and Sees High Engagement: Quilt.AI and AWARE Study,' AWARE, January 17, 2022, https://www.aware.org.sg/2021/09/online-misogyny-quilt-ai-aware-study/.